W9-CKF-178

WORD ROOTS

Level 1

Learning the Building Blocks of Better Spelling and Vocabulary

Word Roots products available in print, software, or eBook form.

Word Roots Series

• Beginning • Level 1 • Level 2 • Level 3 • Level 4

Flashcards: Beginning • Level 1 • Level 2 • Level 3

Written by
Cherie A. Plant

Edited by
Patricia Gray

Graphic Design by
Chip Dombrowski
Scott Slyter

© 2015, 2012, 2002
THE CRITICAL THINKING CO.™
www.CriticalThinking.com
Phone: 800-458-4849 • Fax: 541-756-1758
1991 Sherman Ave., Suite 200 • North Bend • OR 97459
ISBN 978-1-60144-671-8

Table of Contents

About the Author

A graduate in Elementary Education with a minor in Latin from the City University of New York, Cherie Plant is an accomplished etymologist (one who studies the origin and derivation of words). While teaching, Plant found that children as young as seven were fascinated with decoding words such as "triskaidekaphobia" (fear of the number 13) using the knowledge of prefixes, suffixes, and root words.

Plant retired from teaching in 1995, but was convinced that other youngsters could benefit from such study. She has since devoted her time to writing language materials for all age groups, based on the study of Latin and Greek roots.

Introduction

"A mind is like a parachute; it works best when it is open."

— Lord Thomas Dewar

Word Roots is designed to help students expand their spelling, vocabulary, and comprehension skills. *Word Roots* is a uniquely designed and challenging workbook based on the word elements: roots, prefixes, and suffixes. Note that the roots used in this book originate from both the Latin and Greek languages—the foundation of much of our English language.

Roots, prefixes, and suffixes are the building blocks upon which all words are formed. A thorough knowledge of these elements will greatly enhance one's vocabulary and improve one's understanding of otherwise unfamiliar words. For example, understanding the meaning of the roots **struct**, **spect**, **frag**, **nov**, **manu**, and **script** would enable one to comprehend many words made from combinations of these elements, such as the following:

fragment	inscription	prospect
fragile	manuscript	manual
innovation	destruction	construct

A single Latin or Greek root can be the basis for many words in the English language. The significance of this lies in the fact that with every new root learned, the resulting growth of one's vocabulary can be truly astounding—and *Word Roots* provides the tools.

Etymology

Etymology is the study of the origin and the historical development of a word. It explains the earliest known use of a word, its transition from one language to another, and how it changed in form and meaning over time. Therefore, when reference is being made to "the etymology of a word," it means the origin of that particular word.

The word **etymology** itself is derived from the Greek word **etymologia**. The root **etymon** means *true* and the suffix **-logia** means *the study of*. **Etymon** is also used in English to refer to the root of a given word. For example, the Latin word **candidus**, which means *pure, white, sincere*, is the etymon of the English word **candid** which means *honest, frank*.

The Difference Between the Definition of a Word and the Etymology of a Word

The definition of a word tells us what a word means and how it is currently used. The etymology of a word tells us where a word came from, which was often from another language, and what it once meant.

For example, the dictionary definition of the word **disaster** is *any happening that causes great harm or damage; serious or sudden misfortune; a catastrophe*. However, the etymology of the word **disaster** refers back in time when people would blame great calamities on the influence of the stars.

Through etymology we discover that in the late 16th century, Shakespeare used the word in the play *King Lear*. It derived from the Old Italian word **disastro**, which meant *unfavorable to one's stars*.

This antiquated, astrological reference to the word **disaster** is easier to understand when we study the Latin root **astr**, meaning *star*, which is also in our modern word **astronomy**. When the Latin prefix **dis-**, meaning *apart, opposite of*, is added to the root, **astr**, the word (in Old Italian, Latin, and Middle French) conveyed the idea that a catastrophe was traceable to the *evil influence of a star* (a definition that is now obsolete in modern dictionaries). The definitions of many words have changed over time, and the older meanings have slowly disappeared.

Another example is our English word **salary,** which is defined in the dictionary as *fixed payment to a person at regular intervals for services rendered*. The word's etymology can be traced back 2,000 years to the Latin word **sal** meaning *salt*.

There doesn't seem to be much of a connection between our English word **salary** and the Latin word for salt. However, by means of etymology we discover that in ancient Rome, part of a Roman soldier's pay was with salt, which was widely used as a food preservative back then.

Over time, the word **sal** evolved into the word **salarium** which signified *compensation paid in any form, usually monetary*. We still hear the expression used today, "worth your salt," which essentially means *a person is hardworking and earning his salary*. Nonetheless, this is only an expression, and it doesn't mean that salt is the true definition of salary.

Why Knowledge of the Origin of a Word Is Important

Although our English language derives from Old English, or Anglo-Saxon, the majority of the words used in modern English have evolved from many languages—mainly Latin and Greek. Knowing the language of origin of a word is an invaluable tool when it comes to the correct spelling of a word (orthography). As an example, knowing that the sound of /f/ in a word of Greek origin is spelled with a **ph** will help you to correctly spell words such as **biography**, **photograph**, and **telephone**.

Also, knowing that the root for **ten** is spelled **deka** in Greek, but is spelled **dec/deca** in Latin will help with the spelling of words of Greek origin, such as **dekan** and **triskaidekaphobia**, and words of Latin origin, such as **decimal**, **decagon**, and **duodecennial**.

Why Words Are Fun

Knowing how words have evolved over time can teach you a great deal about our culture. Studying the etymology of familiar words can help you deduce the meanings of unfamiliar words, thus enriching your vocabulary. Lastly, hearing stories about the history of words can be very interesting, exciting, and thought provoking.

Definitions of Root, Prefix, and Suffix

A **root** is the element that gives the basic meaning of the word. In this book, the term root refers to the original Latin or Greek word. An English word may have two or more roots in it. Identifying these roots can help you to define a word you don't know.

A **prefix** is an element that is added to the beginning of a root. The prefix adds to, or alters, the meaning of the word.

    Prefix: **re-** means *back, again*
    Prefix: **con-** means *with or together*
    Root: **tract** means *to draw or pull*
        re- + tract = retract: *to draw or pull back*
        con- + tract = contract: *to draw together or shrink*

A **suffix** is an element added to the end of a root. The suffix adds to or alters the meaning of the word.

    Root: **dur** means *harden, to last, lasting*
    Suffix: **-able** means *able to be*
    Suffix: **-ation** means *an action or process*
        dur + -able = durable: *having the quality of lasting*
        dur + -ation = duration: *the length of time something lasts*

Words such as convention and digression have both a prefix and a suffix joined to the root.

Word and Word Parts

The information below will help you identify the word elements (parts).
- Some roots do not need a prefix or suffix to form a word.
    act, tract, script, herb
- A word can have more than one root.
    manu + script = manuscript
- A word can have more than one prefix.
    in- + e- + lig + -ible = ineligible
- A word can have a prefix and a suffix.
    re- + puls + -ive = repulsive
- A word can have more than one suffix
    funct + -ion + -less = functionless
- In some words, connecting vowels and/or consonants are used to join word parts or to complete a word. For the sake of simplicity, connecting vowels and consonants used to join word parts or to complete words will appear in gray.
    herb + i + cide = herbicide
    fer + t + ile = fertile
    medi + at + or = mediator
    de + scribe = describe
- In some cases, to help smooth the sound of the spoken word, a vowel is added to a root. This vowel (usually an o), is referred to as a connecting vowel, and the modified root is called a combining form. For example, the root **hydr** uses the connecting vowel o to produce the combining form hydro, which then combines with the root **electr** and the suffix **-ic** to form the word hydroelectric. In the lessons, an asterisk (*) is used to indicate if a root is a combining form.
    hydr + o = hydro (combining form)
    hydro + electr + ic = hydroelectric
- Some roots are considered to be combining forms, yet do not follow the general rule. The last letter of a root or suffix may be dropped when a suffix is added.
    mob + -ile + -ity   –ile drops the e = mobility

Pretest/Posttest

Before starting *Word Roots*, test your existing knowledge of word meanings. On the blank spaces provided, write what you think each word means. After you complete the book, take the test again on a separate sheet of paper and compare your answers from before and after to determine the progress you've made.

1. traverse _____

2. regression _____

3. brevity _____

4. contradict _____

5. pugnacious _____

6. postscript _____

7. cumulative _____

8. accelerate _____

9. animate _____

10. emissary _____

11. loquacious _____

12. envision _____

13. vociferous _____

14. veracity _____

15. infraction _____

Lesson 1

PREFIX		ROOT		SUFFIX	
con-	with, together	struct	build	-ion	an action or process; state, quality, act
de-	from, away, down, apart; not			-ure	state, quality, act; that which; process, condition
infra-	beneath				
ob-	to, toward, against				
re-	back, again				

A. Spelling and Defining Words

Write each word from the choice box next to its definition.

> destruction ✓   destruct ✓   infrastructure ✓   construct ✓
> reconstruct ✓   reconstruction ✓   structure   construction ✓
> obstruction ✓   obstruct ✓

1. _destruct_ — to deliberately destroy an object

2. _infrastructure_ — underlying framework of a system

3. _construction_ — the action or process of building

4. _destruction_ — the act of destroying; a state of damage

5. _reconstruct_ — to put back together again

6. _structure_ — that which is built in a particular way

7. _obstruction_ — an obstacle put up against something else

8. _reconstruction_ — the act of putting back together

9. _obstruct_ — to block or fill with obstacles

10. _construct_ — to form by putting together parts

B. Completing the Sentence
Write the best word from the gray box to complete each sentence.

1. The hurricane that struck the Florida coast caused a great deal of _d_____.

   reconstruction　destruction✓　obstruction

2. The accident on the highway was a major _____ to the flow of traffic.

   structure　construction　obstruction✓

3. Jeremy kept busy all afternoon with the _____ of his Lego® tower from the fallen pieces.

   destruction　reconstruction✓　construction

4. The _____ of a school consists of teachers, administration, and a school board.

   infrastructure✓　construction　structure✓

5. He was hoping to _____ the new model airplane within a week.

   destruct　construct✓　reconstruct

6. The _____ of the new bridge took two years.

   construction✓　destruction　obstruction

7. A large _____ is being erected on the old fairground site.

   infrastructure　obstruction　structure✓

8. If the dead tree should fall it will _____ the road.

   obstruct✓　construct　destruct

9. In the science fiction movie, the plan was to _____ the space vehicle.

   structure　destruction　destruct✓

10. In order to solve the case, the detective had to _____ the crime scene.

   reconstruct✓　structure　obstruct

C. Defining the Word Parts

Write the definition from the choice box next to its correct word part.

- • beneath ✓
- • an action or process; state, quality, act
- • build
- • to, toward, against
- • with, together
- • back, again
- • from, away, down, apart; not
- • state, quality, act; that which; process, condition
- • for, before, forward

1. -ion   _____

2. struct   _____

3. re-   _____

4. de-   _____

5. infra-   beneath _____

6. -ure   _____

7. con-   _____

8. ob-   _____

D. Writing Sentences

Use each word from the choice box to write a sentence in context so that its meaning is clear to the reader.

For example: I like to construct things. (*unclear; no context*)

I like to construct buildings by stacking blocks on top of each other. (*clear*)

destruction	obstruction	reconstruction	infrastructure	construct
reconstruct	destruct	obstruct	structure	construction

1. The destructionn of the building was so cool because it was satisfing

2. a fallen tree was the cause of the obstruction on the road

3. I had to reconstruct my lego house because it was unstable

4.

5.

6.

7.

8.

9.

10.

E. (optional) Creative Writing

Use some or all of the words from the choice box to write one or more paragraphs or a short story on a separate piece of paper.

Lesson 2

PREFIX	
con-	with, together
ex-	out, away, from
in-	in, into; not
re-	back, again

ROOT	
tract	to draw or pull, drag, draw out
vinc/ vince	conquer

SUFFIX	
-ible	able to be
-ion	an action or process; state, quality, act

A. Spelling and Defining Words

Write each word from the choice box next to its definition.

> contract   retract   convincible   extraction
> extractible   convince   contraction   retraction
> extract   invincible

1. _____   to pull or draw out from

2. _____   to draw together

3. _____   able to be pulled or drawn out from

4. _____   process of withdrawing; pulling out

5. _____   unbeatable; impossible to overcome

6. _____   to persuade by argument or evidence

7. _____   able to be conquered; able to be made to agree with

8. _____   to draw or pull back

9. _____   process of pulling back

10. _____   act of drawing together or shrinking

B. Completing the Sentence
Write the best word from the gray box to complete each sentence.

1. Bridges must be built to withstand the expansion and _____ caused by the weather.

    retraction   contraction   extraction

2. The attorney tried to _____ the jury that the defendant was not guilty.

    convince   contract   retract

3. The tooth _____ was done by an oral surgeon.

    contraction   retraction   extraction

4. The brave troops were trained to march forth as though they were _____.

    invincible   convincible   extractible

5. Cindy wished she could _____ what she said, but her friends had already heard it.

    extract   contract   retract

6. When you bend your elbow, the muscles of the arm _____.

    retract   contract   extract

7. We use our juicer to _____ the nutrients from fruits and vegetables.

    contract   retract   extract

8. The gum was _____ from her hair using WD-40®.

    invincible   extractible   convincible

9. Most people are _____ when presented with reliable facts.

    convincible   invincible   extractible

10. The newspaper had to print a/an _____ after it stated, "pandas eat wood."

    contraction   extraction   retraction

C. Defining the Word Parts

Write the definition from the choice box next to its correct word part.

- conquer
- with, together
- an action or process; state, quality, act
- out, away, from
- between, among
- to draw or pull, drag, draw out
- in, into; not
- back, again
- able to be

1. in- _____

2. tract _____

3. -ion _____

4. con- _____

5. -ible _____

6. vinc/vince _____

7. ex- _____

8. re- _____

D. Writing Sentences

Use each word from the choice box to write a sentence in context so that its meaning is clear to the reader.

contract	extract	convince	convincible	extraction
extractible	retract	invincible	contraction	retraction

1. _____

   _____

   _____

2. _____

   _____

   _____

3. _____

   _____

   _____

4. _____

   _____

   _____

5. _____

   _____

   _____

6. _____

   _____

   _____

7. _____

   _____

   _____

8. _____

   _____

   _____

9. _____

   _____

   _____

10. _____

   _____

   _____

E. (optional) Creative Writing

Use some or all of the words from the choice box to write one or more paragraphs or a short story on a separate piece of paper.

Review
Lessons 1 and 2

A. Write each word part from the choice box next to its definition.

con-	ex-	ob-	-ure	vinc/vince
de-	in-	-ible	struct	aud
re-	infra-	-ion	tract	

1. _____ back, again

2. _____ to, toward, against

3. _____ from, away, down, apart; not

4. _____ with, together

5. _____ out, away, from

6. _____ beneath

7. _____ in, into; not

8. _____ able to be

9. _____ conquer

10. _____ an action or process; state, quality, act

11. _____ build

12. _____ to draw or pull, drag, draw out

13. _____ state, quality, act; that which; process, condition

B. Write the letter of the correct definition for each word.

WORD		DEFINITION
1. infrastructure	_____	(a) that which is built in a particular way
2. obstruction	_____	(b) able to be pulled or drawn out from
3. convincible	_____	(c) act of drawing together or shrinking
4. construct	_____	(d) to persuade by argument or evidence
5. structure	_____	(e) process of withdrawing; pulling out
6. retraction	_____	(f) the act of putting back together
7. extractible	_____	(g) to block or fill with obstacles
8. construction	_____	(h) the act of destroying; a state of damage
9. contraction	_____	(i) underlying framework of a system
10. invincible	_____	(j) to pull or draw out from
11. retract	_____	(k) to form by putting together parts
12. convince	_____	(l) to draw together
13. extraction	_____	(m) to put back together again
14. destruction	_____	(n) able to be conquered; able to be made to agree with
15. reconstruction	_____	(o) to deliberately destroy an object
16. extract	_____	(p) an obstacle put up against something else
17. contract	_____	(q) the action or process of building
18. obstruct	_____	(r) to draw or pull back
19. destruct	_____	(s) unbeatable; impossible to overcome
20. reconstruct	_____	(t) process of pulling back

C. Use the jumbled letters to write the correct word for each definition.

JUMBLED LETTERS	DEFINITION	WORD
1. icntncoeoutrsr	the act of putting back together	_____
2. cotanoncrti	act of drawing together or shrinking	_____
3. linicinebv	unbeatable; impossible to overcome	_____
4. oustbctr	to block or fill with obstacles	_____
5. ttericoanr	process of pulling back	_____
6. itcoxenrta	process of withdrawing; pulling out	_____
7. crctstuon	to form by putting together parts	_____
8. rcuesrttu	that which is built in a particular way	_____
9. necovcni	to persuade by argument or evidence	_____
10. rettrca	to draw or pull back	_____
11. etielbxatrc	able to be pulled or drawn out from	_____
12. tonrtnuicsoc	the action or process of building	_____
13. trurcfeiarsntu	underlying framework of a system	_____
14. ncorcstture	to put back together again	_____
15. ilebnciocnv	able to be conquered; able to be made to agree with	_____
16. uridncoetst	the act of destroying; a state of damage	_____
17. tactrnco	to draw together	_____
18. cnbtsuirtoo	an obstacle put up against something else	_____
19. xetactr	to pull or draw out from	_____
20. dcrtutes	to deliberately destroy an object	_____

D. Write the best word from the gray box to complete each sentence.

1. The _____ in her throat caused her to stop breathing.

   structure   obstruction   retraction

2. The city ordered the _____ of the old building since it was beyond repair.

   destruction   construction   reconstruction

3. The giant believed he was _____ until Jack chopped down the beanstalk.

   convincible   invincible   contractible

4. The _____ being built is the new library.

   obstruction   infrastructure   structure

5. Nolan always manages to _____ some humor from every situation.

   extract   contract   retract

6. The _____ of a democracy is based on the principle: "of the people, by the people, for the people."

   destruction   infrastructure   reconstruction

7. I think you should _____ that statement unless you can defend it with some facts.

   retract   extract   obstruct

8. The _____ of the new office building took the builders six months to complete.

   destruction   construction   reconstruction

9. The voters were not _____ despite the politician's lengthy speech.

   invincible   contractible   convincible

10. The police asked the witness to _____ the robbery scene from beginning to end.

   reconstruct   retract   structure

11. Rosa had everything she needed to _____ a nice new tree house for her

three children.

construct   obstruct   reconstruct

12. Grandpa asked the newspaper to print a/an _____ of his death notice.

contraction   extraction   retraction

13. A considerable number of medicines are _____ from rain forest plants.

contractible   extractible   invincible

14. When forming a _____ from two words, what form of punctuation is used?

contraction   retraction   reconstruction

15. Neither of the men could _____ the other of his beliefs regarding Bigfoot.

obstruct   contract   convince

16. My dad has to go to a special dentist for the _____ of a decayed tooth.

extraction   retraction   construction

17. Jon went for _____ of his leg following a war injury.

construction   retraction   reconstruction

18. A snail will _____ its muscles in order to glide forward on its own slime.

extract   construct   contract

19. The group planned to _____ the entrance to the computer store that had

cheated them.

obstruct   destruct   construct

20. NASA was certain the satellite wouldn't _____ upon re-entry to Earth.

retract   obstruct   destruct

Lesson 3

PREFIX	
com-	with, together
im-	in, into; not
pro-	for, before, forward
re-	back, again

ROOT	
mob/ mot/ mote/ mov	move

SUFFIX	
-able	able to be
-ile	like, of, relating to
-ion	an action or process; state, quality, act
il-ity	state, quality, act

A. Spelling and Defining Words

Write each word from the choice box next to its definition.

> immobility   movable   immobile   immovable
> commotion   removable   promotion   mobile
> promote   mobility

1. _____ able to be taken or carried away

2. _____ the scene of noisy confusion or activity

3. _____ motionless; unable to move

4. _____ an advancement in rank or position

5. _____ relating to the quality of being able to move

6. _____ unable to move or be moved; fixed; immobile

7. _____ able to be moved from one place to another

8. _____ relating to the quality of not being able to move

9. _____ to move forward or raise to a higher rank, class, status, etc.

10. _____ relating to being able to move; movable

B. Completing the Sentence
Write the best word from the gray box to complete each sentence.

1. The _____ locomotive was in need of repair.

    > mobile   movable   immobile

2. The cat would have more _____ outside the cage.

    > mobility   commotion   immobility

3. Mason's _____ was due to his commitment to his work.

    > immobility   promotion   mobility

4. The entrance was blocked by a/an _____ boulder.

    > immovable   removable   movable

5. Mia woke up from a sound sleep due to the _____ outside her tent.

    > promotion   immobility   commotion

6. The winter coat has a/an _____ lining that zips out.

    > immovable   movable   removable

7. The military was planning to _____ the corporal to sergeant.

    > promote   immobile   removable

8. Leo's _____ was due to a serious back injury.

    > promotion   mobility   immobility

9. Our living room furniture is lightweight and easily _____.

    > immovable   movable   immobile

10. Six weeks after her knee surgery, Kerry was _____ again.

    > mobile   movable   immobile

C. Defining the Word Parts

Write the definition from the choice box next to its correct word part.

> - state, quality, act
> - with, together
> - move
> - break
> - back, again
> - in, into; not
> - like, of, relating to
> - for, before, forward
> - an action or process; state, quality, act
> - able to be

1. re- _____

2. -able _____

3. com- _____

4. im- _____

5. -ile _____

6. pro- _____

7. -ion _____

8. mob/mot/
    mote/mov _____

9. il-ity _____

D. Writing Sentences
Use each word from the choice box to write a sentence in context so that its meaning is clear to the reader.

| movable | promote | immobile | promotion | removable |
| commotion | immovable | mobile | mobility | immobility |

1. _____

_____

_____

2. _____

_____

_____

3. _____

_____

_____

4. _____

_____

_____

5. _____

_____

_____

6. _____

_____

_____

7. _____

_____

_____

8. _____

_____

_____

9. _____

_____

_____

10. _____

_____

_____

E. (optional) Creative Writing
Use some or all of the words from the choice box to write one or more paragraphs or a short story on a separate piece of paper.

Lesson 4

PREFIX		ROOT		SUFFIX	
ab-	away, from	brev	short	-able	able to be
ac-	to, toward, near	cede/ceed/cess	go, yield	i-ate	to make, to act; one who, that which
pro-	for, before, forward			-ible	able to be
se-	apart, aside			-ion	an action or process; state, quality, act
				-ity	state, quality, act

A. Spelling and Defining Words

Write each word from the choice box next to its definition.

> accessible   secession   procession   processable
> brevity   abbreviate   proceed   accede
> process   secede

1. _____ to shorten

2. _____ a method of doing or producing something

3. _____ the act of formally withdrawing from a group

4. _____ quality of being brief; shortness in time

5. _____ easily entered, approached, or obtained

6. _____ to go forward, especially after stopping

7. _____ to formally break away from

8. _____ the act of going forward in an orderly manner

9. _____ able to be subjected to a series of actions that yield a change

10. _____ to agree; to yield to

B. Completing the Sentence

Write the best word from the gray box to complete each sentence.

1. The neighborhood was unhappy with the government and attempted to

    _____ from the city.   accede   proceed   secede

2. The ice skaters were warned to _____ with caution on the rough ice rink.

    proceed   secede   process

3. Scraps of paper are _____ into a slurry which has artistic applications.

    processable   accessible   procession

4. The students learned how to _____ the names of the states.

    process   secede   abbreviate

5. Since the cookie jar was on the kitchen counter and not on a high shelf, the children found it

    was easily _____.   accessible   processable   proceed

6. Jorje's father had to _____ to his son's wish to attend the college of his

    choice.   secede   accede   proceed

7. Mom made apple butter by the _____ of boiling apples down and adding

    sugar and spices.   process   procession   secession

8. Following the Confederacy's _____ from the Union, the Civil War broke out.

    procession   secession   process

9. The audience was tired and appreciated the _____ of the politician's speech.

    secession   brevity   procession

10. The _____ moved slowly down Main Street.

    secession   brevity   procession

C. Defining the Word Parts
Write the definition from the choice box next to its correct word part.

- short
- able to be
- away, from
- go, yield
- to, toward, near
- back, again
- state, quality, act
- for, before, forward
- apart, aside
- an action or process; state, quality, act
- to make, to act; one who, that which

1. -able   _____

2. ab-   _____

3. brev   _____

4. ac-   _____

5. -ion   _____

6. pro-   _____

7. -ible   _____

8. cede/ceed/
cess   _____

9. se-   _____

10. i-ate   _____

11. -ity/il-ity   _____

D. Writing Sentences

Use each word from the choice box to write a sentence in context so that its meaning is clear to the reader.

accessible	process	abbreviate	procession	processable
brevity	secession	secede	proceed	accede

1. _____

2. _____

3. _____

4. _____

5. _____

6. _____

7. _____

8. _____

9. _____

10. _____

E. (optional) Creative Writing

Use some or all of the words from the choice box to write one or more paragraphs or a short story on a separate piece of paper.

Review
Lessons 3 and 4

A. Write each word part from the choice box next to its definition.

com-	re-	se-	i-ate	de-	mob/mot/mote/mov
im-	ab-	-able	-ible	-ile	-ity/il-ity
pro-	ac-	-ion	brev		cede/ceed/cess

1. _____ back, again

2. _____ to, toward, near

3. _____ to make, to act; one who, that which

4. _____ with, together

5. _____ away, from

6. _____ in, into; not

7. _____ able to be

8. _____ move

9. _____ an action or process; state, quality, act

10. _____ like, of, relating to

11. _____ for, before, forward

12. _____ apart, aside

13. _____ able to be

14. _____ short

15. _____ go, yield

16. _____ state, quality, act

B. Write the letter of the correct definition for each word.

WORD		DEFINITION
1. commotion _____	(a)	able to be taken or carried away
2. immobile _____	(b)	unable to move or be moved; fixed; immobile
3. promotion _____	(c)	the act of formally withdrawing from a group
4. removable _____	(d)	able to be subjected to a series of actions that yield a change
5. mobility _____	(e)	to formally break away from
6. secede _____	(f)	relating to the quality of being able to move
7. abbreviate _____	(g)	the act of going forward in an orderly manner
8. proceed _____	(h)	the scene of noisy confusion or activity
9. brevity _____	(i)	relating to the quality of not being able to move
10. accessible _____	(j)	able to be moved from one place to another
11. immobility _____	(k)	quality of being brief; shortness in time
12. promote _____	(l)	to shorten
13. movable _____	(m)	motionless; unable to move
14. processable _____	(n)	to agree; to yield to
15. accede _____	(o)	relating to being able to move; movable
16. process _____	(p)	to go forward, especially after stopping
17. secession _____	(q)	to move forward or raise to a higher rank, class, status, etc.
18. immovable _____	(r)	a method of doing or producing something
19. procession _____	(s)	easily entered, approached, or obtained
20. mobile _____	(t)	an advancement in rank or position

C. Use the jumbled letters to write the correct word for each definition.

JUMBLED LETTERS	DEFINITION	WORD
1. rncsiposoe	the act of going forward in an orderly manner	_____
2. ertopom	to move forward or raise to a higher rank, class, status, etc.	_____
3. oelbmi	relating to being able to move; movable	_____
4. tomoocnmi	the scene of noisy confusion or activity	_____
5. oieimlmb	motionless; unable to move	_____
6. prsbsloeace	able to be subjected to a series of actions that yield a change	_____
7. blmievamo	unable to move or be moved; fixed; immobile	_____
8. ooprotnim	an advancement in rank or position	_____
9. essosnice	the act of formally withdrawing from a group	_____
10. vbaremelo	able to be taken or carried away	_____
11. toylbimi	relating to the quality of being able to move	_____
12. rcepsos	a method of doing or producing something	_____
13. eecesd	to formally break away from	_____
14. bteaaeibvr	to shorten	_____
15. eoerpdc	to go forward, especially after stopping	_____
16. ivbetyr	quality of being brief; shortness in time	_____
17. ibscesaelc	easily entered, approached, or obtained	_____
18. eadcce	to agree; to yield to	_____
19. mimibitylo	relating to the quality of not being able to move	_____
20. elmbavo	able to be moved from one place to another	_____

D. Write the best word from the gray box to complete each sentence.

1. The art assistant was surprised to hear of her _____ to head artist.

   processable promotion procession

2. The transit system became _____ due to extreme blizzard conditions.

   immobile invincible accessible

3. Because of the _____ of the first ball game, he was able to stay for the

   second one.   commotion brevity contraction

4. Hector converted his van into a/an _____ snack bar.

   promote immobile mobile

5. The company ran an advertising campaign to _____ its new products.

   process promote construct

6. The teacher asked the class what the _____ was all about.

   procession immobility commotion

7. It was months after the accident that Ivy gained her _____ back.

   mobility brevity immobility

8. You can _____ the word "Mister" as "Mr."

   promote abbreviate process

9. The principal was always _____ to the students.

   accessible processable removable

10. My GPS directed me to _____ to the next light, then turn left.

    accede secede proceed

D. (continued) Write the best word from the gray box to complete each sentence.

11. Sawyer found the _____ of his vehicle to be very upsetting.

     immobility   brevity   obstruction

12. My brother's toy fire truck had many _____ parts.

     movable   extractible   accessible

13. The tab on the medicine bottle was _____, but only with a strong twist.

     accessible   removable   immovable

14. From 1860-1861, eleven states voted to _____ from the United States.

     secede   proceed   accede

15. The yams weren't _____ because they were too old.

     removable   immobile   processable

16. The funeral _____ included fellow marines carrying her casket.

     procession   commotion   secession

17. Could it be that nothing is truly _____ as long as a stronger force exists?

     movable   immovable   removable

18. In January 2014, Catalonia voted for _____ from Spain.

     secession   brevity   procession

19. Learning is a _____ that includes memorization and application.

     commotion   process   procession

20. Katherine had to _____ that Raold's sculpture was the best.

     accede   secede   proceed

Lesson 5

PREFIX		ROOT		SUFFIX	
ac-	to, toward, near	**celer**	fast	**-ate**	to make, to act; one who, that which
de-	from, away, down, apart; not	**gress**	step	**-ation**	an action or process
di-	apart, away; not			**-ion**	an action or process; state, quality, act
pro-	for, before, forward				
re-	back, again				

A. Spelling and Defining Words

Write each word from the choice box next to its definition.

progression	decelerate	deceleration	progress
accelerate	regress	digression	regression
digress	acceleration		

1. _____   to reduce the speed of

2. _____   a departure from the main issue, subject, etc.

3. _____   a movement forward or onward; improvement

4. _____   a movement back to an earlier state

5. _____   to increase the speed of

6. _____   to depart from the main issue, subject, etc.

7. _____   the action or process of reducing the speed of

8. _____   to go back to an earlier state

9. _____   the process or action of moving forward

10. _____   the action or process of increasing the speed of

B. Completing the Sentence
Write the best word from the gray box to complete each sentence.

1. As the car approached the icy curve, the driver needed to _____.

    digress   accelerate   decelerate

2. The student's _____ from the book topic annoyed the teacher.

    digression   progression   regression

3. The contractor was hoping to _____ the building process so the office complex would be finished before winter started.

    decelerate   accelerate   progress

4. The teacher was happy to see the _____ his class had made in learning multiplication.

    regression   progress   deceleration

5. The illness had caused a gradual _____ in his ability to speak.

    digression   acceleration   regression

6. To _____, to deviate, and to wander from the topic all mean the same thing.

    digress   progress   regress

7. We watched an amazing parade with a _____ of more and more elaborate floats.

    regression   progression   digression

8. Which pedal does the driver press down on for the _____ of a vehicle?

    acceleration   regression   digression

9. Let me _____ to the point we were discussing earlier.

    progress   digress   regress

10. The _____ of her car was very obvious as she entered the school zone.

    regression   deceleration   progression

C. Defining the Word Parts
Write the definition from the choice box next to its correct word part.

> - to make, to act; one who, that which
> - fast
> - to, toward, near
> - an action or process
> - apart, away; not
> - back, again
>
> - state, quality, act
> - for, before, forward
> - step
> - from, away, down, apart; not
> - an action or process; state, quality, act

1. -ion　　_____

2. ac-　　_____

3. celer　　_____

4. -ate　　_____

5. gress　　_____

6. re-　　_____

7. pro-　　_____

8. de-　　_____

9. -ation　　_____

10. di-　　_____

D. Writing Sentences

Use each word from the choice box to write a sentence in context so that its meaning is clear to the reader.

progression	digress	regress	deceleration	progress
accelerate	decelerate	acceleration	digression	regression

1. _____

_____

_____

2. _____

_____

_____

3. _____

_____

_____

4. _____

_____

_____

5. _____

_____

_____

6. _____

_____

_____

7. _____

_____

_____

8. _____

_____

_____

9. _____

_____

_____

10. _____

_____

_____

E. (optional) Creative Writing

Use some or all of the words from the choice box to write one or more paragraphs or a short story on a separate piece of paper.

Lesson 6

PREFIX		ROOT		SUFFIX	
com-	with, together	**avi/** **avia**	bird	**-able**	able to be
		memor	remember	**i-al**	like, related to; an action or process
				-ary	that which; someone or something that belongs to; of, related to; one who
				-ate	to make, to act; one who, that which
				-ation/ **iz-ation**	an action or process
				at-or	one who, that which; condition, state, activity
				-ize	to make, to act
				-trix	feminine
				-y	state of, quality, act; body, group

A. Spelling and Defining Words

Write each word from the choice box next to its definition.

> aviary   aviation   memorize   memorization
> aviatrix   memory   memorable   commemorate
> aviator   memorial

1. _____ related to remembering a person or event

2. _____ a large enclosure in which birds are kept

3. _____ a woman airplane pilot

4. _____ to honor the memory of, as by a ceremony

5. _____ an ability to retain knowledge; an individual's stock of retained knowledge

6. _____ one who flies an airplane; a pilot

7. _____ the act or practice of flying airplanes, helicopters, etc.

8. _____ to learn something so well that you are able to remember it perfectly

9. _____ able to be remembered; worth remembering

10. _____ the process of committing something to memory

B. Completing the Sentence
Write the best word from the gray box to complete each sentence.

1. The highlight of their trip to the zoo was visiting the _____.

    aviator   aviatrix   aviary

2. The veterans of World War II gathered together to _____ those who had died.

    commemorate   memorize   memorable

3. The _____ was famous for her performance of some of the most daring feats ever seen.

    aviary   aviatrix   aviator

4. Cole's head injury caused a partial loss of _____ that lasted for weeks.

    memory   memorization   aviation

5. The family held a _____ service for their grandfather who recently passed away.

    memory   memorial   memorization

6. The history of _____ goes back to a few centuries B.C. when kites and hot air balloons were invented by the Chinese.

    aviation   aviatrix   memorization

7. Have you ever wondered why some advertising jingles are so _____?

    memorial   avairy   memorable

8. Everyone will have to _____ a poem for next week.

    commemorate   memorize   memory

9. In 1837, America's first female _____, Amelia Earhart, attempted a solo flight across the Atlantic.

    aviary   aviation   aviator

10. _____ is an essential part of education, especially when learning the times tables.

    Memorization   Aviation   Commemorate

C. Defining the Word Parts
Write the definition from the choice box next to its correct word part.

> * an action or process
> * able to be
> * with, together
> * bird
> * to make, to act
> * one who, that which; condition, state, activity
> * to make, to act; one who, that which
>
> * like, related to; an action or process
> * remember
> * under, below
> * feminine
> * state of, quality, act; body, group
> * that which; someone or something that belongs to; of, related to; one who

1. i-al   _____

2. memor   _____

3. avi/avia   _____

4. com-   _____

5. -able   _____

6. -ary   _____

7. at-or   _____

8. -trix   _____

9. -ation/ iz-ation   _____

10. -ate   _____

11. -ize   _____

12. -y   _____

D. Writing Sentences

Use each word from the choice box to write a sentence in context so that its meaning is clear to the reader.

aviary	aviator	memory	memorize	memorization
aviatrix	aviation	memorial	memorable	commemorate

1. _____

_____

_____

2. _____

_____

_____

3. _____

_____

_____

4. _____

_____

_____

5. _____

_____

_____

6. _____

_____

_____

7. _____

_____

_____

8. _____

_____

_____

9. _____

_____

_____

10. _____

_____

_____

E. (optional) Creative Writing

Use some or all of the words from the choice box to write one or more paragraphs or a short story on a separate piece of paper.

Review
Lessons 5 and 6

A. Write each word part from the choice box next to its definition.

-ion	-ate	pro-	di-	memor	-able	-trix
ac-	gress	de-	-ine	avi/avia	-ary	-ation/iz-ation
celer	re-	-y	i-al	com-	at-or	-ize

1. _____ to make, to act; one who, that which

2. _____ fast

3. _____ to, toward, near

4. _____ an action or process

5. _____ apart, away; not

6. _____ back, again

7. _____ for, before, forward

8. _____ from, away, down, apart; not

9. _____ an action or process; state, quality, act

10. _____ step

11. _____ able to be

12. _____ an action or process

13. _____ with, together

14. _____ bird

15. _____ one who, that which; condition, state, activity

16. _____ like, related to; an action or process

17. _____ remember

18. _____ feminine

19. _____ state of, quality, act; body, group

20. _____ that which; someone or something that belongs to; of, related to; one who

21. _____ to make, to act

B. Write the letter of the correct definition for each word.

WORD		DEFINITION
1. aviary _____	(a)	an ability to retain knowledge; an individual's stock of retained knowledge
2. memorable _____	(b)	a woman airplane pilot
3. accelerate _____	(c)	to honor the memory of, as by a ceremony
4. aviator _____	(d)	to reduce the speed of
5. progress _____	(e)	a departure from the main issue, subject, etc.
6. commemorate _____	(f)	a movement forward or onward; improvement
7. regress _____	(g)	a large enclosure in which birds are kept
8. memorize _____	(h)	to increase the speed of
9. decelerate _____	(i)	a movement backward to an earlier state
10. aviatrix _____	(j)	related to remembering a person or event
11. memorization _____	(k)	one who flies an airplane; a pilot
12. digression _____	(l)	the act or practice of flying airplanes, helicopters, etc.
13. acceleration _____	(m)	the action or process of reducing the speed of
14. memory _____	(n)	to depart from the main issue, subject, etc.
15. aviation _____	(o)	able to be remembered; worth remembering
16. regression _____	(p)	the process or act of moving forward
17. memorial _____	(q)	to go back to an earlier state
18. deceleration _____	(r)	the action or process of increasing the speed of
19. progression _____	(s)	the process of committing something to memory
20. digress _____	(t)	to learn something so well that you are able to remember it perfectly

C. Use the jumbled letters to write the correct word for each definition.

JUMBLED LETTERS	DEFINITION	WORD
1. rspsogoiren	the process or act of moving forward	_____
2. bmmaloree	able to be remembered; worth remembering	_____
3. cactlaeeer	to increase the speed of	_____
4. ivayar	a large enclosure in which birds are kept	_____
5. segirds	to depart from the main issue, subject, etc.	_____
6. iaiemootnrzm	the process of committing something to memory	_____
7. eeeceatlrd	to reduce the speed of	_____
8. arxviait	a woman airplane pilot	_____
9. rsseger	to go back to an earlier state	_____
10. nieclaroacet	the action or process of increasing the speed of	_____
11. cetreoommma	to honor the memory of, as by a ceremony	_____
12. eroidnssig	a departure from the main issue, subject, etc.	_____
13. narceeoldite	the action or process of reducing the speed of	_____
14. iaatorv	one who flies an airplane; a pilot	_____
15. rmozmiee	to learn something so well that you are able to remember it perfectly	_____
16. sprrgeos	a movement forward or onward; improvement	_____
17. yomrem	an ability to retain knowledge; an individual's stock of retained knowledge	_____
18. anvioiat	the act or practice of flying airplanes, helicopters, etc.	_____
19. gnsrersieo	a movement backward to an earlier state	_____
20. mrlemoia	related to remembering a person or event	_____

D. Write the best word from the gray box to complete each sentence.

1. The _____ contained many tropical birds.

   > aviary   aviatrix   aviator

2. There were thousands of people in attendance at the _____ celebration
   for Dr. Martin Luther King Jr.

   > memorization   memorable   memorial

3. The ice on the tracks caused the conductor to _____ the train when
   approaching curves.

   > decelerate   accelerate   regress

4. The _____ of Ray's mind further into the past was due to old age.

   > digression   progression   regression

5. The _____ worked for United Airlines.

   > aviary   aviatrix   aviation

6. Fertilizer will _____ the growth of the tomato plants.

   > accelerate   decelerate   regress

7. My _____ isn't as good as it used to be.

   > memorization   progression   memory

8. We made swift _____ when climbing the mountain.

   > progress   deceleration   digression

9. The bicentennial will _____ the town's first 200 years.

   > accelerate   decelerate   commemorate

10. Oliver's long _____ made him forget his main point.

   > progression   digression   regression

11. Many scientists link changing weather patterns to the _____ of global

warming.

    acceleration   regression   digression

12. High school graduation is a _____ occasion in everyone's life.

    memorial   memorable   memorization

13. After speaking of his grandfather during the lesson, the teacher said, "However, I

_____ …," then continued with his lecture.

    digress   regress   progress

14. The solo flight from New York to Paris by the _____ Charles Lindbergh

fascinated people worldwide.

    aviatrix   aviary   aviator

15. Since a baby can't read, _____ is the only means he has of learning

language.

    memorization   regression   progression

16. The psychologist sadly observed her patient _____ to his former state

of anxiety.

    digress   progress   regress

17. Satellite communications, GPS, and small but powerful computers have made modern

_____ a safe and affordable means of travel.

    aviary   aviation   progression

18. My uncle was so sure he could _____ the route, he didn't take a map and

got lost.

    memorize   commemorate   accelerate

19. My brother's _____ from owning a canoe to a luxury yacht was a favorite

family topic.

    regression   digression   progression

20. The _____ of the growth of the cancerous tumor pleased the oncologist.

    deceleration   acceleration   progression

Lesson 7

PREFIX	
re-	back, again
sub-	under, below

ROOT	
aqu/ aqua	water
mar	sea
pug/ pugn	fight

SUFFIX	
-acious	having the quality of
-ant	one who, that which; state, quality
-arium	place where
-eous	like, having the quality of
t**-ic**	like, related to
-ine	like, related to
il**-ism**	a state of being, a quality or act
il**-ist**	one who

A. Spelling and Defining Words

Write each word from the choice box next to its definition.

> marine   submarine   pugnacious   aquarium
> repugnant   pugilism   pugilist   aqueous
> aquatic   aquamarine

1. _____ a place where aquatic organisms are kept and exhibited

2. _____ distasteful; offensive or revolting

3. _____ of, or pertaining to the sea

4. _____ one who fights as a profession; boxer

5. _____ being, living, or used under water

6. _____ related to the animals and plants that live in or near water

7. _____ blue-green in color, like sea water

8. _____ having a quarrelsome or aggressive nature

9. _____ the act of boxing

10. _____ like, or having the quality of water; watery

B. Completing the Sentence

Write the best word from the gray box to complete each sentence.

1. Lucy grew up near the ocean, which influenced her to pursue a career in
_____ biology.

aquatic   marine   submarine

2. The man's _____ behavior resulted in his hitting someone.

pugnacious   aquatic   repugnant

3. The _____ canyon in California's Monterey Bay is two miles deep.

aquatic   aqueous   submarine

4. Spitting in public is _____.

pugnacious   repugnant   pugilism

5. The bottom and sides of the swimming pool were painted _____.

aquamarine   marine   aqueous

6. Ducks are _____ creatures.

aqueous   aquatic   pugnacious

7. The _____ had his nose broken on more than one occasion.

pugilist   pugilism   aquarium

8. The first _____ opened in Regent's Park, England, in 1853.

submarine   aquarium   marine

9. The retired boxer wrote a book on the art of _____.

aquamarine   repugnant   pugilism

10. The fish was floating in a/an _____ solution.

aqueous   aquatic   marine

C. Defining the Word Parts

Write the definition from the choice box next to its correct word part. A definition may be used more than once.

> • having the quality of
> • like, related to
> • water
> • back, again
> • with, together
> • act, state, condition
> • one who
>
> • sea
> • under, below
> • place where
> • one who, that which; state, quality
> • like, having the quality of
> • fight

1. t-ic _____

2. re- _____

3. -arium _____

4. -eous _____

5. pug/pugn _____

6. sub- _____

7. -acious _____

8. -ant _____

9. aqu/aqua _____

10. il-ism _____

11. -ine _____

12. mar _____

13. il-ist _____

D. Writing Sentences

Use each word from the choice box to write a sentence in context so that its meaning is clear to the reader.

marine	aquatic	pugilism	pugnacious	aquarium
repugnant	submarine	aquamarine	pugilist	aqueous

1. _____

   _____

   _____

2. _____

   _____

   _____

3. _____

   _____

   _____

4. _____

   _____

   _____

5. _____

   _____

   _____

6. _____

   _____

   _____

7. _____

   _____

   _____

8. _____

   _____

   _____

9. _____

   _____

   _____

10. _____

   _____

   _____

E. (optional) Creative Writing

Use some or all of the words from the choice box to write one or more paragraphs or a short story on a separate piece of paper.

Lesson 8

PREFIX	
counter-	against, opposite
in-	in, into; not
inter-	between, among
re-	back, again

ROOT	
act	to do, to drive
aud	hear

SUFFIX	
i-ence	state, quality, act
-ible	able to be
-ion	an action or process; state, quality, act

A. Spelling and Defining Words

Write each word from the choice box next to its definition.

> inaudible   interaction   inaction   audible
> counteract   reaction   react   counteraction
> audience   interact

1. _____   unable to be heard

2. _____   to act directly against; to prevent from affecting

3. _____   a response

4. _____   communication between two or more people or things

5. _____   a group of listeners or spectators

6. _____   able to be heard

7. _____   to act in return or reciprocally

8. _____   the act of going directly against

9. _____   to talk or do things with others

10. _____   the state of not doing something that should be done; idleness

B. Completing the Sentence
Write the best word from the gray box to complete each sentence.

1. Elas's _____ to the surprise birthday party was one of shock.

    inaction   reaction   interaction

2. There was a great deal of positive _____ among the classmates.

    interaction   reaction   counteraction

3. Comedians perform best with a live _____.

    audience   interaction   reaction

4. The doctor advised his patient to drink plenty of water to _____ the
dehydrating effects of the medication.

    react   interact   counteract

5. The children were talking so quietly that they were almost _____.

    audible   inaudible   inaction

6. Sometimes, _____ is necessary, especially when one is ill.

    inaction   interaction   counteraction

7. Ruby's loud yawn was _____ throughout the entire room.

    reaction   inaudible   audible

8. The firemen had to _____ quickly when the alarm sounded.

    interact   react   counteract

9. It was easy for the new student to _____ with the other children.

    react   counteract   interact

10. Vitamin K is used in the _____ of certain drugs that are used to prevent
blood clots.

    counteraction   interaction   inaction

C. Defining the Word Parts
Write the definition from the choice box next to its correct word part.

> - state, quality, act
> - against, opposite
> - to do, to drive
> - able to be
> - back, again
> - in, into; not
> - having the quality of
> - an action or process; state, quality, act
> - between, among
> - hear

1. -ion   _____

2. in-   _____

3. aud   _____

4. counter-   _____

5. act   _____

6. -ible   _____

7. i-ence   _____

8. inter-   _____

9. re-   _____

D. Writing Sentences

Use each word from the choice box to write a sentence in context so that its meaning is clear to the reader.

| inaudible | audience | reaction | inaction | audible |
| counteract | interaction | interact | react | counteraction |

1. _____

_____

_____

2. _____

_____

_____

3. _____

_____

_____

4. _____

_____

_____

5. _____

_____

_____

6. _____

_____

_____

7. _____

_____

_____

8. _____

_____

_____

9. _____

_____

_____

10. _____

_____

_____

E. (optional) Creative Writing

Use some or all of the words from the choice box to write one or more paragraphs or a short story on a separate piece of paper.

Review
Lessons 7 and 8

A. Write each word part from the choice box next to its definition.

in-	aqu/aqua	i-ence	-ion	mar	-ant	il-ism	pro-
-ible	act	-arium	inter-	-acious	-ine	il-ist	t-ic
sub-	counter-	re-	aud	pug/pugn	-eous		

1. _____ having the quality of

2. _____ like, related to

3. _____ water

4. _____ back, again

5. _____ between, among

6. _____ a state of being, a quality or act

7. _____ one who

8. _____ sea

9. _____ under, below

10. _____ place where

11. _____ one who, that which; state, quality

12. _____ like, related to

13. _____ like, having the quality of

14. _____ fight

15. _____ state, quality, act

16. _____ against, opposite

17. _____ to do, to drive

18. _____ able to be

19. _____ in, into; not

20. _____ hear

21. _____ an action or process; state, quality, act

B. Write the letter of the correct definition for each word.

WORD		DEFINITION
1. interaction _____	(a)	a place where aquatic organisms are kept and exhibited
2. audience _____	(b)	distasteful; offensive or revolting
3. pugnacious _____	(c)	of, or pertaining to the sea
4. audible _____	(d)	one who fights as a profession; boxer
5. react _____	(e)	being, living, or used under water
6. aqueous _____	(f)	unable to be heard
7. inaction _____	(g)	to act directly against; to prevent from affecting
8. pugilism _____	(h)	a response
9. aquarium _____	(i)	communication between two or more people or things
10. repugnant _____	(j)	a group of listeners or spectators
11. interact _____	(k)	related to the animals and plants that live in or near water
12. counteraction _____	(l)	blue-green in color, like sea water
13. marine _____	(m)	having a quarrelsome or aggressive nature
14. reaction _____	(n)	the act of boxing
15. inaudible _____	(o)	like, or having the quality of water; watery
16. pugilist _____	(p)	able to be heard
17. submarine _____	(q)	act in return or reciprocally
18. aquamarine _____	(r)	the act of going directly against
19. aquatic _____	(s)	to talk or do things with others
20. counteract _____	(t)	the state of not doing something that should be done; idleness

C. Use the jumbled letters to write the correct word for each definition.

JUMBLED LETTERS	DEFINITION	WORD
1. uouesqa	like, or having the quality of water; watery	_____
2. uatrpnneg	distasteful; offensive or revolting	_____
3. ooreitnncactu	the act of going directly against	_____
4. eulaibd	able to be heard	_____
5. rineam	of, or pertaining to the sea	_____
6. tiqacua	related to the animals and plants that live in or near water	_____
7. pmiglius	the act of boxing	_____
8. cetotnairin	communication between two or more people or things	_____
9. eaiudnec	a group of listeners or spectators	_____
10. eqiuamaran	blue-green in color, like sea water	_____
11. ptsluigi	one who fights as a profession; boxer	_____
12. mqiuauar	a place where aquatic organisms are kept and exhibited	_____
13. tecucotarn	to act directly against; to prevent from affecting	_____
14. ueibildan	unable to be heard	_____
15. eatrc	to act in return or reciprocally	_____
16. neaisubrm	being, living, or used under water	_____
17. anontici	the state of not doing something that should be done; idleness	_____
18. acrientt	to talk or do things with others	_____
19. cguaosnpiu	having a quarrelsome or aggressive nature	_____
20. nairetoc	a response	_____

D. Write the best word from the gray box to complete each sentence.

1. Mrs. Miller taught the children that chewing with their mouths open was
   _____.   pugnacious repugnant inaudible

2. The teacher was pleased to observe the good _____ among the
   science teammates.   interaction reaction counteraction

3. The school's _____ to discipline the disruptive students angered
   many parents.   interaction reaction inaction

4. The primary requirement for maintaining _____ organisms is good
   water quality.   submarine aquatic repugnant

5. The music was barely _____.
                                   audible repugnant inaudible

6. When Jeff didn't like someone, he'd become quite _____.
                                   repugnant inaudible pugnacious

7. The _____ applauded the amazing performance.
                                   audience pugilist marine

8. My school has an excellent course in _____ biology.
                                   aquamarine submarine marine

9. My sister's _____ contains many exotic fishes.
                                   aquarium submarine audience

10. Water prompts the _____ of iron and oxygen to become rust.
                                   counteraction reaction inaction

D. (continued) Write the best word from the gray box to complete each sentence.

11. How do you think she'll _____ when you propose marriage?

react   interact   counteract

12. The students examined the _____ fossils found in coral reefs.

aquamarine   submarine   aqueous

13. Animals can hear sounds that are _____ to humans.

audible   repugnant   inaudible

14. It's hard to _____ when you don't speak the same language.

interact   counteract   react

15. The _____ was in the heavyweight category.

audience   submarine   pugilist

16. The _____ necklace she wore matched the color of her eyes.

aquamarine   marine   aqueous

17. Tylenol® will _____ her high fever.

react   interact   counteract

18. Henry worked diligently to perfect the art of _____.

pugilism   counteraction   interaction

19. When we studied the lens of the eye, we learned about the _____ humor.

aquatic   marine   aqueous

20. The doctor prescribed medication for the _____ of chronic fatigue.

interaction   reaction   counteraction

Lesson 9

PREFIX	
circum-	around
con-	with, together
inter-	between, among
re-	back, again

ROOT	
juven	young
vene/ vent	come

SUFFIX	
-ate	to make, to act; one who, that which
-ile	like, of, relating to
-ion	an action or process; state, quality, act
-ive	tending to or performing

A. Spelling and Defining Words

Write each word from the choice box next to its definition.

intervene	rejuvenate	intervention	convention
juvenile	convent	circumventive	circumvent
circumvention	convene		

1. _____   youthful or childish; immature

2. _____   to bring back to youthful strength or appearance

3. _____   to go around; to bypass restrictions

4. _____   a gathering or assembly of people with a common interest

5. _____   to come between; to intercede

6. _____   process of going around; the act of bypassing restrictions

7. _____   religious house where a community of nuns reside

8. _____   to meet together; assemble

9. _____   the action of coming between; act of interceding

10. _____   tending to go around; tending to bypass restrictions

B. Completing the Sentence

Write the best word from the gray box to complete each sentence.

1. Noah attempted to _____ the no-hats rule at school by wearing a sun visor.

   rejuvenate   convene   circumvent

2. The bus driver was forced to _____ when two passengers began shouting at each other.

   convene   intervene   circumvent

3. The aging beauty queen was hopeful that cosmetic surgery would _____ her looks.

   rejuvenate   circumvent   intervene

4. The mother thought her teen daughter's temper tantrum in public showed _____ behavior.

   convene   circumventive   juvenile

5. Scientists from all over the world attended the annual _____.

   convention   intervention   circumvention

6. "This book is awesome," said Lily, so she decided to _____ a group for a book discussion.

   convene   intervene   circumvent

7. Without the lawyer's _____, an innocent person would have gone to jail.

   convention   intervention   circumvention

8. A nun lives in a _____, while a monk lives in a monastery.

   convention   circumvention   convent

9. With the enemy in the valley, it was easy to take a _____ approach to defeat them.

   convent   circumventive   juvenile

10. The parade route included the _____ of the large water fountain downtown.

    convention   circumvention   intervention

C. Defining the Word Parts

Write the definition from the choice box next to its correct word part.

> - with, together
> - around
> - to do, to drive
> - to make, to act; one who, that which
> - young
> - between, among
>
> - like, of, relating to
> - tending to or performing
> - come
> - back, again
> - an action or process; state, quality, act

1. re- _____

2. juven _____

3. -ate _____

4. circum- _____

5. vene/vent _____

6. -ile _____

7. con- _____

8. inter- _____

9. -ion _____

10. -ive _____

D. Writing Sentences

Use each word from the choice box to write a sentence in context so that its meaning is clear to the reader.

| intervene | circumvention | convent | intervention | convention |
| juvenile | rejuvenate | convene | circumventive | circumvent |

1. _____

   _____

   _____

2. _____

   _____

   _____

3. _____

   _____

   _____

4. _____

   _____

   _____

5. _____

   _____

   _____

6. _____

   _____

   _____

7. _____

   _____

   _____

8. _____

   _____

   _____

9. _____

   _____

   _____

10. _____

    _____

    _____

E. (optional) Creative Writing

Use some or all of the words from the choice box to write one or more paragraphs or a short story on a separate piece of paper.

Lesson 10

PREFIX	
de-	from, away, down, apart; not
ex-	out, away, from
re-	back, again

ROOT	
cogn	know
termin	end, limit

SUFFIX	
-al	like, related to; an action or process
iz-ant	one who, that which; state, quality
-ate	to make, to act; one who, that which
-ation	an action or process
it-ive	tending to or performing
-ize	to make, to act
i-tion	state, quality, act

A. Spelling and Defining Words

Write each word from the choice box next to its definition.

> cognition   exterminate   extermination   cognitive
> recognize   terminal   recognition   cognizant
> determination   terminate

1. _____   to identify someone or something seen before

2. _____   process of acquiring knowledge

3. _____   to destroy or get rid of completely

4. _____   an intent to reach a goal

5. _____   related to something leading to the end or to death

6. _____   having intellectual activity, as in thinking and reasoning

7. _____   act of acknowledging or noticing

8. _____   the state of being aware or informed of something

9. _____   process of destroying or getting rid of completely

10. _____   to bring to an end

B. Completing the Sentence

Write the best word from the gray box to complete each sentence.

1. The child recovered from the illness the doctors had said was _____.

    cognitive   terminal   cognizant

2. Dan's _____ to win every race got him to the Olympics.

    determination   recognition   cognition

3. Since they hadn't seen each other in many years, the former classmates failed to
    _____ each other.

    terminate   exterminate   recognize

4. I called a pest control company to _____ the fleas in our house.

    exterminate   recognize   terminate

5. Scientists have studied the brains of infants and their _____

    determination   cognition   recognition

6. Gordon was pretty upset that his boss decided to _____ him as a
    company employee.

    terminate   recognize   exterminate

7. Overhunting in the 1860s nearly caused the _____ of buffalo in the U.S.

    recognition   cognition   extermination

8. Georgette received widespread _____ for rescuing the family from their
    burning home.

    cognition   recognition   determination

9. Katie was _____ of the basic job requirements before she went for her
    interview.

    cognizant   cognitive   terminal

10. After the crash, James suffered terrible physical as well as _____
    disabilities.

    terminal   cognitive   cognizant

C. Defining the Word Parts

Write the definition from the choice box next to its correct word part.

> - out, away, from
> - like, related to; an action or process
> - from, away, down, apart; not
> - know
> - to make, to act; one who, that which
> - back, again
> - having the quality of
>
> - an action or process
> - end, limit
> - to make, to act
> - state, quality, act
> - one who, that which; state, quality
> - tending to or performing

1. iz-ant _____

2. de- _____

3. cogn _____

4. -al _____

5. re- _____

6. it-ive _____

7. termin _____

8. -ate _____

9. ex- _____

10. -ize _____

11. i-tion _____

12. -ation _____

D. Writing Sentences

Use each word from the choice box to write a sentence in context so that its meaning is clear to the reader.

cognition	determination	terminal	extermination	cognitive
recognize	exterminate	terminate	recognition	cognizant

1. _____

_____

_____

2. _____

_____

_____

3. _____

_____

_____

4. _____

_____

_____

5. _____

_____

_____

6. _____

_____

_____

7. _____

_____

_____

8. _____

_____

_____

9. _____

_____

_____

10. _____

_____

_____

E. (optional) Creative Writing

Use some or all of the words from the choice box to write one or more paragraphs or a short story on a separate piece of paper.

Review
Lessons 9 and 10

A. Write each word part from the choice box next to its definition.

juven	-ion	circum-	inter-	i-tion	iz-ant	ex-
-ate	re-	con-	i-ence	-ize	-al	termin
de-	-ile	vene/vent	-ation	cogn	-ive/it-ive	

1. _____ an action or process

2. _____ end, limit

3. _____ to make, to act

4. _____ state, quality, act

5. _____ one who, that which; state, quality

6. _____ tending to or performing

7. _____ young

8. _____ between, among

9. _____ like, of, relating to

10. _____ come

11. _____ back, again

12. _____ an action or process; state, quality, act

13. _____ out, away, from

14. _____ like, related to; an action or process

15. _____ from, away, down, apart; not

16. _____ know

17. _____ to make, to act; one who, that which

18. _____ with, together

19. _____ around

B. Write the letter of the correct meaning for each word.

WORD	DEFINITION
1. terminal _____	(a) process of going around; the act of bypassing restrictions
2. juvenile _____	(b) religious house where a community of nuns reside
3. circumvent _____	(c) to meet together; assemble
4. intervene _____	(d) to identify someone or something seen before
5. cognizant _____	(e) process of acquiring knowledge
6. cognitive _____	(f) to destroy or get rid of completely
7. recognition _____	(g) an intent to reach a goal
8. circumvention _____	(h) related to something leading to the end or to death
9. terminate _____	(i) the action of coming between; act of interceding
10. extermination _____	(j) tending to go around; tending to bypass restrictions
11. convent _____	(k) youthful or childish; immature
12. convention _____	(l) to bring back to youthful strength or appearance
13. convene _____	(m) to go around; to bypass restrictions
14. rejuvenate _____	(n) a gathering or assembly of people with a common interest
15. recognize _____	(o) to come between; to intercede
16. exterminate _____	(p) having intellectual activity, as in thinking and reasoning
17. determination _____	(q) act of acknowledging or noticing
18. cognition _____	(r) the state of being aware or informed of something
19. circumventive _____	(s) process of destroying or getting rid of completely
20. intervention _____	(t) to bring to an end

C. Use the jumbled letters to write the correct word for each definition.

JUMBLED LETTERS	DEFINITION	WORD
1. oicginotn	process of acquiring knowledge	_____
2. trmiaetne	to bring to an end	_____
3. veijleun	youthful or childish; immature	_____
4. etnruoncmivic	process of going around; the act of bypassing restrictions	_____
5. igeonrezc	to identify someone or something seen before	_____
6. atimntioenxre	process of destroying or getting rid of completely	_____
7. itocngiev	having intellectual activity, as in thinking and reasoning	_____
8. atjneeruev	to bring back to youthful strength or appearance	_____
9. cterucmivn	to go around; to bypass restrictions	_____
10. cenevno	to meet together; assemble	_____
11. arinemtonedti	an intent to reach a goal	_____
12. erinnocoitg	act of acknowledging or noticing	_____
13. lainmtre	related to something leading to the end or to death	_____
14. entnrevie	to come between; to intercede	_____
15. nencvot	religious house where a community of nuns reside	_____
16. ntcioznga	the state of being aware or informed of something	_____
17. emirnaxtete	to destroy or get rid of completely	_____
18. ioonvtcnne	a gathering or assembly of people with a common interest	_____
19. vecricvnimteu	tending to go around; tending to bypass restrictions	_____
20. nivntnotiree	the action of coming between; act of interceding	_____

D. Write the best word from the gray box to complete each sentence.

1. Elliot's _____ to improve his grades was evident in his report card.

   > cognition   determination   circumvention

2. A good night's rest helped _____ the overworked accountant.

   > rejuvenate   convene   terminate

3. Ant traps helped us _____ the ants taking over the kitchen.

   > circumvent   terminate   exterminate

4. The garden club will _____ on the first Monday of each month.

   > convene   intervene   terminate

5. Maisie's storytelling was so _____ that no one could follow what was going on.

   > juvenile   circumventive   cognitive

6. By 1970, the _____ of wolves for the purpose of protecting farmland was widespread in the United States.

   > extermination   recognition   intervention

7. The citizens are fully _____ of the governor's many theories about why our state is bankrupt.

   > cognitive   juvenile   cognizant

8. The local _____ runs a food bank to help the needy in the community.

   > convent   intervention   cognition

9. So far, no animal has been discovered with the _____ capacity of the human.

   > juvenile   cognizant   cognitive

10. I didn't _____ you in that disguise.

    > recognize   circumvent   terminate

11. Many artists gain _____ after death.

> cognition   recognition   circumvention

12. For a grown man, he acted in a very _____ manner.

> cognitive   juvenile   circumventive

13. The con artist tried to _____ the law.

> terminate   intervene   circumvent

14. The referee had to _____ before the players hurt each other.

> intervene   convene   circumvent

15. The lease will _____ in June.

> convene   terminate   rejuvenate

16. If it weren't for Jack's quick _____ of the tree, he might have had a terrible accident.

> circumvention   intervention   recognition

17. The Republican presidential candidate will be chosen at the national _____.

> intervention   convention   recognition

18. Main Street is the _____ stop for this bus route.

> circumventive   cognizant   terminal

19. The policeman's _____ broke up the fight.

> determination   intervention   recognition

20. Following a concussion, her _____ became permanently impaired.

> cognition   determination   recognition

Lesson 11

PREFIX	
circum-	around
de-	from, away, down, apart; not
in-	in, into; not
post-	after
pre-	before, in front of

ROOT	
scribe/ script	write, written

SUFFIX	
-ion	an action or process; state, quality, act
-ive	tending to or performing

A. Spelling and Defining Words

Write each word from the choice box next to its definition.

circumscribe   postscript   prescribe   inscribe

describe   prescription   description   descriptive

inscription   circumscriptive

1. _____   to represent with words or pictures

2. _____   a written order for medicine

3. _____   an engraving on a coin or other object

4. _____   to draw around; to encircle

5. _____   an addition to an already completed letter, article, or book

6. _____   tending to limit or enclose; restrictive

7. _____   to write or set down as a rule, order, or direction; to order or advise as a medicine

8. _____   action or process of picturing in words

9. _____   to write or engrave on some surface

10. _____   tending to put forth in words

B. Completing the Sentence

Write the best word from the gray box to complete each sentence.

1. Lila squeezed in a/an _____ at the bottom of her letter telling the date of
   her return.

   inscription description postscript

2. The math class was learning to _____ various geometric figures
   with a compass.

   circumscribe inscribe prescribe

3. The _____ on the medallion showed the date of her birthday.

   prescription description inscription

4. The nurse called the pharmacy with the _____ for the patient's medicine.

   description prescription inscription

5. Alice asked me to _____ a sea otter because she had never seen one.

   describe prescribe inscribe

6. The farmer had to plant his crops within the _____ boundaries of
   his property.

   descriptive circumscriptive inscription

7. From Hillary's _____ the farmhouse seems very rustic.

   description inscription circumscriptive

8. Kelly was sure the vet would _____ an antibiotic for her dog's bursitis.

   inscribe prescribe describe

9. He told the jeweler, "_____ the ring: Love always, Randy."

   Inscribe Describe Prescribe

10. The author is so _____, a reader can almost smell the flowers.

    inscription circumscriptive descriptive

C. Defining the Word Parts
Write the definition from the choice box next to its correct word part.

> - around
> - write, written
> - an action or process; state, quality, act
> - from, away, down, apart; not
> - tending to or performing
> - in, into; not
> - go, yield
> - after
> - before, in front of

1. de- _____

2. -ive _____

3. scribe/script _____

4. circum- _____

5. in- _____

6. pre- _____

7. -ion _____

8. post- _____

D. Writing Sentences

Use each word from the choice box to write a sentence in context so that its meaning is clear to the reader.

circumscribe	inscription	prescription	prescribe	inscribe
describe	postscript	circumscriptive	description	descriptive

1. _____

   _____

   _____

2. _____

   _____

   _____

3. _____

   _____

   _____

4. _____

   _____

   _____

5. _____

   _____

   _____

6. _____

   _____

   _____

7. _____

   _____

   _____

8. _____

   _____

   _____

9. _____

   _____

   _____

10. _____

   _____

   _____

E. (optional) Creative Writing

Use some or all of the words from the choice box to write one or more paragraphs or a short story on a separate piece of paper.

Lesson 12

PREFIX	
con-	with, together
in-	in, into; not
inter-	between, among
re-	back, again

ROOT	
capt/ cept	take, hold
tact	touch

SUFFIX	
-ile	like, of, relating to
-ive	tending to or performing
-or	one who, that which, condition, state, activity
-ure	state, quality, act, that which; process, condition

A. Spelling and Defining Words

Write each word from the choice box next to its definition.

intercept	intact	receptive	receptor
recapture	tactile	interceptor	interceptive
contact	capture		

1. _____ the state of touching or meeting

2. _____ of, or relating to the sense of touch

3. _____ to stop or interrupt the course of

4. _____ the taking back of something

5. _____ with nothing missing; left whole

6. _____ the act of taking or being taken by force

7. _____ tending to receive; take in, admit, contain

8. _____ that which holds or receives (in various senses)

9. _____ a person or thing that stops or interrupts the course of

10. _____ tending to stop or interrupt the course of

B. Completing the Sentence

Write the best word from the gray box to complete each sentence.

1. The package arrived torn, but the things inside were _____.

    > receptive   intact   tactile

2. The authorities announced the _____ of the escaped prisoners.

    > recapture   receptor   interceptor

3. The soccer player was trying to _____ a forward pass.

    > capture   recapture   intercept

4. On _____ the wallpaper stuck to the wall.

    > intact   contact   receptor

5. A blind person uses _____ objects to learn what something looks like.

    > tactile   intact   interceptive

6. The _____ of the white whale was Captain Ahab's obsession.

    > recapture   contact   capture

7. The clients were very _____ to the ad agency's presentation.

    > receptive   interceptive   tactile

8. As a talented athlete, Jake was a valued _____ of football passes.

    > receptor   contact   interceptor

9. The signal didn't reach the TV because the _____ was blocked.

    > interceptor   receptor   contact

10. _____ action by fighter planes was ordered when an unidentified aircraft entered U.S. airspace.

    > Receptive   Interceptive   Tactile

C. Defining the Word Parts

Write the definition from the choice box next to its correct word part.

> - tending to or performing
> - touch
> - with, together
> - back, again
> - like, of, relating to
> - one who, that which; condition, state, activity
>
> - in, into; not
> - take, hold
> - between, among
> - out, away, from
> - state, quality, act, that which; process, condition

1. -ile _____

2. con- _____

3. tact _____

4. -ure _____

5. in- _____

6. -ive _____

7. re- _____

8. inter- _____

9. capt/cept _____

10. -or _____

D. Writing Sentences

Use each word from the choice box to write a sentence in context so that its meaning is clear to the reader.

intercept	contact	tactile	receptive	receptor
recapture	intact	capture	interceptor	interceptive

1. _____

   _____

   _____

2. _____

   _____

   _____

3. _____

   _____

   _____

4. _____

   _____

   _____

5. _____

   _____

   _____

6. _____

   _____

   _____

7. _____

   _____

   _____

8. _____

   _____

   _____

9. _____

   _____

   _____

10. _____

   _____

   _____

E. (optional) Creative Writing

Use some or all of the words from the choice box to write one or more paragraphs or a short story on a separate piece of paper.

Review
Lessons 11 and 12

A. Write each word part from the choice box next to its definition.

-ion	-ive	circum-	-ure	re-	pre-
con-	in-	de-	inter-	capt/cept	brev
scribe/script	-ile	tact	-or	post-	

1. _____ around

2. _____ write, written

3. _____ an action or process; state, quality, act

4. _____ from, away, down, apart; not

5. _____ with, together

6. _____ take, hold

7. _____ like, of, relating to

8. _____ in, into; not

9. _____ between, among

10. _____ touch

11. _____ state, quality, act, that which; process, condition

12. _____ back, again

13. _____ after

14. _____ before, in front of

15. _____ tending to or performing

16. _____ one who, that which; condition, state, activity

B. Write the letter of the correct definition for each word.

WORD		DEFINITION
1. intact _____	a	to write or set down as a rule, order, or direction; to order or advise as a medicine
2. capture _____	b	action or process of picturing in words
3. interceptive _____	c	to write or engrave on some surface
4. circumscriptive _____	d	tending to put forth in words
5. inscription _____	e	the state of touching or meeting
6. recapture _____	f	of, or relating to the sense of touch
7. receptive _____	g	to stop or interrupt the course of
8. tactile _____	h	the taking back of something
9. prescribe _____	i	with nothing missing; left whole
10. circumscribe _____	j	to represent with words or pictures
11. describe _____	k	a written order for medicine
12. contact _____	l	an engraving on a coin or other object
13. postscript _____	m	to draw around; to encircle
14. prescription _____	n	an addition to an already completed letter, article, or book
15. descriptive _____	o	tending to limit or enclose; restrictive
16. description _____	p	the act of taking or being taken by force
17. intercept _____	q	tending to receive; take in, admit, contain
18. interceptor _____	r	that which holds or receives (in various senses)
19. receptor _____	s	a person or thing that stops or interrupts the course of
20. inscribe _____	t	tending to stop or interrupt the course of

C. Use the jumbled letters to write the correct word for each definition.

	JUMBLED LETTERS	DEFINITION	WORD
1.	cinsebri	to write or engrave on some surface	_____
2.	ctipresvide	tending to put forth in words	_____
3.	rectnetip	to stop or interrupt the course of	_____
4.	cteuperar	the taking back of something	_____
5.	ittecla	of, or relating to the sense of touch	_____
6.	rerpcoet	that which holds or receives (in various senses)	_____
7.	ieriscmbccru	to draw around; to encircle	_____
8.	iicertpsndo	action or process of picturing in words	_____
9.	ocstptisrp	an addition to an already completed letter, article, or book	_____
10.	oantctc	the state of touching or meeting	_____
11.	uaectpr	the act of taking or being taken by force	_____
12.	ietiteerncvp	tending to stop or interrupt the course of	_____
13.	ciatnt	with nothing missing; left whole	_____
14.	icrpevtee	tending to receive; take in, admit, contain	_____
15.	sebirdce	to represent with words or pictures	_____
16.	siorncntipi	an engraving on a coin or other object	_____
17.	ceiebrsrp	to write or set down as a rule, order, or direction; to order or advise as a medicine	_____
18.	ticsreonirpp	a written order for medicine	_____
19.	notprcertei	a person or thing that stops or interrupts the course of	_____
20.	rrvcsmctciiiupe	tending to limit or enclose; restrictive	_____

D. Write the best word from the gray box to complete each sentence.

1. Mom and Dad gave a complete _____ of everything that was stolen.

   inscription   description   prescription

2. The _____ of the skunk in our backyard was a huge relief to Mom.

   capture   recapture   inscription

3. "I'm _____ to hearing your views," John stated, "but I may not agree with you."

   interceptive   circumscriptive   receptive

4. The _____ on the old gravestone was almost unreadable.

   inscription   postscript   receptor

5. Marianne was surprised that the vase was still _____ after it fell off the counter.

   receptive   intact   descriptive

6. A student tried to _____ the note Sue was passing to Sean.

   capture   intercept   inscribe

7. Adjectives and adverbs are _____ words that tell more about nouns and verbs.

   receptive   interceptive   descriptive

8. When Maria changed her car's oil, she used a bowl as a/an _____ for the used oil.

   receptor   interceptor   inscription

9. I will _____ my amazing journey to you in vivid detail.

   inscribe   describe   prescribe

10. It's likely drones will carry _____ missiles to protect the United States from foreign attack.

    interceptive   tactile   receptive

D. (continued) Write the best word from the gray box to complete each sentence.

11. The car turned over when the rear wheels lost _____ with the road.

intact   contact   description

12. The doctor will most likely _____ lots of rest.

describe   inscribe   prescribe

13. The dramatic brushstrokes give the painting a _____ quality.

tactile   descriptive   receptive

14. I filled my _____ at our local pharmacy.

inscription   prescription   receptor

15. The _____ of their rightful territory is their sole objective.

capture   contact   recapture

16. We intend to _____ Uncle Bill's date of birth and date of death on his tombstone.

inscribe   describe   prescribe

17. I never put a/an _____ on an email.

inscription   postscript   description

18. Please _____ in red all major cities on this map.

inscribe   describe   circumscribe

19. This particular fighter _____ is equipped with sophisticated radar.

inscription   interceptor   description

20. Electronic monitoring bracelets are a/an _____ means to keep check on people who are on probation.

circumscriptive   descriptive   interceptive

Lesson 13

PREFIX	
contra-	against, opposite
cor-	with, together
inter-	between, among
pre-	before, in front of

ROOT	
dict	say, speak
rupt	to break, burst

SUFFIX	
-ion	an action or process; state, quality, act
-ure	state, quality, act; that which; process, condition

A. Spelling and Defining Words

Write each word from the choice box next to its definition.

contradict	interrupt	corrupt	contradiction
prediction	rupture	diction	interruption
corruption	predict		

1. _____ to stop or hinder by breaking in on

2. _____ to express or imply the opposite of

3. _____ a breaking apart or the state of being broken apart

4. _____ a statement foretelling the future

5. _____ a break with what is legally or morally right

6. _____ an action in opposition to another

7. _____ to tell or state a future event; foretell

8. _____ to cause to break with what is legally or morally right

9. _____ the act or manner of expression in words

10. _____ action of stopping or hindering by breaking in on

B. Completing the Sentence
Write the best word from the gray box to complete each sentence.

1. Jack's angry facial expressions _____ his friendly words.

        interrupt   corrupt   contradict

2. The promise of quick wealth led to widespread _____ in the city government.

        corruption   contradiction   interruption

3. An earthquake caused the _____ of the underground pipe.

        rupture   interruption   prediction

4. Ella made a _____ that her candidate would win the election.

        contradiction   prediction   corruption

5. The referee was forced to _____ the soccer game because of a sudden hailstorm.

        corrupt   predict   interrupt

6. I _____ that you will get straight A's this semester.

        predict   contradict   interrupt

7. Criminal friends can _____ others and lead them astray.

        interrupt   corrupt   contradict

8. The _____ was caused by a group of hecklers.

        interruption   contradiction   corruption

9. The actor was told to improve his _____.

        prediction   contradiction   diction

10. The instructor wouldn't listen to any _____ of his opinions.

        interruption   contradiction   corruption

C. Defining the Word Parts
Write the definition from the choice box next to its correct word part.

> • against, opposite
> • with, together
> • say, speak
> • for, before, forward
> • to break, burst
>
> • an action or process; state, quality, act
> • between, among
> • before, in front of
> • state, quality, act; that which; process, condition

1. pre-   _____

2. rupt   _____

3. cor-   _____

4. -ion   _____

5. inter-   _____

6. dict   _____

7. -ure   _____

8. contra-   _____

D. Writing Sentences
Use each word from the choice box to write a sentence in context so that its meaning is clear to the reader.

| contradict | corruption | rupture | corrupt | contradiction |
| prediction | interrupt | predict | diction | interruption |

1. _____

_____

_____

2. _____

_____

_____

3. _____

_____

_____

4. _____

_____

_____

5. _____

_____

_____

6. _____

_____

_____

7. _____

_____

_____

8. _____

_____

_____

9. _____

_____

_____

10. _____

_____

_____

E. (optional) Creative Writing
Use some or all of the words from the choice box to write one or more paragraphs or a short story on a separate piece of paper.

Lesson 14

PREFIX	
com-	with, together
de-	from, away, down, apart; not
ex-	out, away, from
im-	in, into; not
op-	to, toward, against

ROOT	
pose/ posit	place, put

SUFFIX	
-ion	an action or process; state, quality, act

A. Spelling and Defining Words

Write each word from the choice box next to its definition.

deposit	expose	oppose	impose
imposition	composition	deposition	exposition
opposition	compose		

1. _____ an excessive or unjust burden placed on someone

2. _____ to put down or in a safe place

3. _____ an arrangement or putting together of parts

4. _____ the act of resistance or action against

5. _____ to place something where it can be seen; to put in an unprotected situation

6. _____ the act of putting down or depositing; the removing from power

7. _____ to act in opposition to; to put against

8. _____ to put together or arrange in proper order

9. _____ a writing or speaking that puts forth or explains

10. _____ to put an excessive or unjust burden on someone

B. Completing the Sentence

Write the best word from the gray box to complete each sentence.

1. The pirates were careful not to _____ the treasure's location.

    deposit   expose   impose

2. The candidate faced strong _____ to his program.

    deposition   imposition   opposition

3. The storm is expected to _____ twenty inches of snow.

    impose   deposit   expose

4. Rachel won first place for her musical _____.

    composition   exposition   deposition

5. Austin felt that asking his neighbor to take him to work was too much of a/an

    _____.

    opposition   deposition   imposition

6. The famous poet hopes to _____ a new sonnet.

    compose   expose   oppose

7. Chase was the only representative to _____ the project.

    impose   compose   oppose

8. The mayor decided to _____ a curfew on the entire city until the

    disturbance was over.

    oppose   impose   compose

9. The _____ of Charles I took place in 1649.

    exposition   deposition   opposition

10. The candidate gave a clear _____ of his policies.

    exposition   composition   imposition

C. Defining the Word Parts
Write the definition from the choice box next to its correct word part.

> - with, together
> - place, put
> - an action or process; state, quality, act
> - from, away, down, apart; not
>
> - out, away, from
> - in, into; not
> - to, toward, against
> - state, quality, act

1. ex-   _____

2. op-   _____

3. -ion   _____

4. com-   _____

5. pose/posit _____

6. de-   _____

7. im-   _____

D. Writing Sentences

Use each word from the choice box to write a sentence in context so that its meaning is clear to the reader.

deposit	opposition	composition	oppose	impose
imposition	expose	compose	deposition	exposition

1. _____

_____

_____

2. _____

_____

_____

3. _____

_____

_____

4. _____

_____

_____

5. _____

_____

_____

6. _____

_____

_____

7. _____

_____

_____

8. _____

_____

_____

9. _____

_____

_____

10. _____

_____

_____

E. (optional) Creative Writing

Use some or all of the words from the choice box to write one or more paragraphs or a short story on a separate piece of paper.

Review
Lessons 13 and 14

A. Write each word part from the choice box next to its definition.

com-	pre-	-ile	contra-	inter-
-ion	-ure	de-	cor-	ex-
dict	pose/posit	im-	rupt	op-

1. _____ with, together

2. _____ place, put

3. _____ an action or process; state, quality, act

4. _____ with, together

5. _____ say, speak

6. _____ to break, burst

7. _____ state, quality, act; that which; process, condition

8. _____ from, away, down, apart; not

9. _____ out, away, from

10. _____ in, into; not

11. _____ to, toward, against

12. _____ against, opposite

13. _____ between, among

14. _____ before, in front of

B. Write the letter of the correct definition for each word.

WORD	DEFINITION
1. corrupt _____	(a) to stop or hinder by breaking in on
2. expose _____	(b) to express or imply the opposite of
3. exposition _____	(c) a breaking apart or the state of being broken apart
4. compose _____	(d) a statement foretelling the future
5. deposit _____	(e) a break with what is legally or morally right
6. composition _____	(f) an action in opposition to another
7. deposition _____	(g) to tell or state a future event; foretell
8. interrupt _____	(h) to cause to break with what is legally or morally right
9. oppose _____	(i) the act or manner of expression in words
10. impose _____	(j) action of stopping or hindering by breaking in on
11. opposition _____	(k) an excessive or unjust burden placed on someone
12. corruption _____	(l) to put down or in a safe place
13. contradiction _____	(m) an arrangement or putting together of parts
14. imposition _____	(n) the act of resistance or action against
15. contradict _____	(o) to place something where it can be seen; to put in an unprotected situation
16. predict _____	(p) the act of putting down or depositing; the removing from power
17. diction _____	(q) to act in opposition to; to put against
18. prediction _____	(r) to put together or arrange in proper order
19. rupture _____	(s) a writing or speaking that puts forth or explains
20. interruption _____	(t) to put an excessive or unjust burden on someone

C. Use the jumbled letters to write the correct word for each definition.

JUMBLED LETTERS	DEFINITION	WORD
1. pcmoeos	to put together or arrange in proper order	_____
2. redipct	to tell or state a future event; foretell	_____
3. pooxnitsei	a writing or speaking that puts forth or explains	_____
4. cootntanrdici	an action in opposition to another	_____
5. empsio	to put an excessive or unjust burden on someone	_____
6. euinrtiptonr	action of stopping or hindering by breaking in on	_____
7. eotnispido	the act of putting down or depositing; the removing from power	_____
8. cdnioit	the act or manner of expression in words	_____
9. soppeo	to act in opposition to; to put against	_____
10. rcutpor	to cause to break with what is legally or morally right	_____
11. dtianctocr	to express or imply the opposite of	_____
12. epseox	to place something where it can be seen; to put in an unprotected situation	_____
13. roepicitdn	a statement foretelling the future	_____
14. osminiptcoo	an arrangement or putting together of parts	_____
15. opncroriut	a break with what is legally or morally right	_____
16. poesdit	to put down or in a safe place	_____
17. tuirntrpe	to stop or hinder by breaking in on	_____
18. miosipinot	an excessive or unjust burden placed on someone	_____
19. rpuetur	a breaking apart or the state of being broken apart	_____
20. iptpnosooi	the act of resistance or action against	_____

D. Write the best word from the gray box to complete each sentence.

1. The town's decision to open a new shopping mall met with a great deal of
   _____.   contradiction   imposition   opposition

2. The teenager felt it was a great _____ to have to clean his room once
   a month.   imposition   exposition   interruption

3. Nat didn't want to _____ his friend Joan, but he felt he must tell the truth.
                  interrupt   contradict   corrupt

4. Poor _____ ruined the effectiveness of Hayley's speech.
                  composition   diction   deposition

5. Ryan's story was in direct _____ to hers.
                  contradiction   imposition   deposition

6. The music students will _____ a song to play at the next assembly.
                  oppose   expose   compose

7. It's uncanny, but Zoey's _____ did come true.
                  prediction   contradiction   imposition

8. A/An _____ in the water main flooded the street.
                  composition   rupture   interruption

9. The commander didn't want to _____ the troops unnecessarily.
                  oppose   corrupt   expose

10. The _____ of brass includes copper and zinc.
                  composition   exposition   deposition

11. _____ your lunch tray at the cafeteria door.

Expose   Deposit   Oppose

12. Our police department seems to be free of _____.

opposition   interruption   corruption

13. I wouldn't even try to _____ the outcome of the election.

predict   expose   interrupt

14. The _____ of the game show was due to a news flash.

corruption   interruption   opposition

15. Sea walls _____ the long stretch of beach.

corrupt   deposit   interrupt

16. A computer virus can _____ your files.

corrupt   expose   interrupt

17. Please don't _____ me on this issue.

compose   impose   oppose

18. Leo tried to _____ his wishes on us.

expose   oppose   impose

19. The complex subject matter requires a lengthy _____.

exposition   opposition   imposition

20. There was a huge _____ of soil on the banks of the river.

composition   deposition   exposition

Lesson 15

PREFIX		ROOT		SUFFIX	
in-	in, into; not	**fract/ frag**	break	**-al**	like, related to; an action or process
				-ary	that which; someone or something that belongs to; of, related to; one who
				-ation	an action or process
				-ile	like, of, relating to
				-ion	an action or process; state, quality, act
				il-ity	state, quality, act
				-ment	that which, state, quality, act
				-ure	state, quality, act; that which, process, condition

A. Spelling and Defining Words

Write each word from the choice box next to its definition.

fraction	fragile	fragility	fragmentation
fracture	fragment	fragmentary	fragmental
infraction	fractional		

1. _____   a broken piece

2. _____   a break, crack, or split

3. _____   easily broken; delicate

4. _____   a part or element of a larger whole

5. _____   related to being incomplete or broken

6. _____   related to being very small; insignificant

7. _____   state of delicateness

8. _____   the act of breaking the limits or rules

9. _____   not complete; disconnected

10. _____   process of breaking, cracking, or splitting; that which is broken or divided

B. Completing the Sentence

Write the best word from the gray box to complete each sentence.

1. The once popular cell phone was no longer in demand and was selling at a

   _____ of its former price.   fragment   infraction   fraction

2. The child's _____ was very evident following a serious illness.

   fragility   fragmentation   infraction

3. They recovered only one large _____ of the beautiful vase after it fell.

   fracture   fragment   fraction

4. Bullying in school is a/an _____ of school policy.

   infraction   fracture   fragmentation

5. The bone _____ was clearly visible on the x-ray.

   infraction   fraction   fracture

6. The prosecutor had _____ evidence against the accused.

   fragmentary   fragile   fragmentation

7. The crystal bowl was extremely _____.

   fragmental   fragile   fractional

8. As a result of a concussion, Thomas could only give a _____ account of

   the accident.   fragile   fragmental   fracture

9. The _____ of the bomb upon explosion caused debris to fly in

   all directions.   fracture   fragmentation   fragility

10. The rise in unemployment has been _____.

    fragmental   fractional   fragile

C. Defining the Word Parts

Write the definition from the choice box next to its correct word part.

> - in, into; not
> - break
> - like, of, relating to
> - an action or process; state, quality, act
> - that which, state, quality, act
> - state, quality, act; that which; process, condition
> - like, related to; an action or process
> - that which; someone or something that belongs to; of, related to; one who
> - state, quality, act
> - to, toward, against
> - an action or process

1. il-ity   _____

2. -ation   _____

3. -ure   _____

4. -ment   _____

5. -ion   _____

6. -ile   _____

7. -al   _____

8. -ary   _____

9. in-   _____

10. fract/frag   _____

D. Writing Sentences

Use each word from the choice box to write a sentence in context so that its meaning is clear to the reader.

fraction	infraction	fragment	fragility	fragmentation
fracture	fragile	fractional	fragmentary	fragmental

1. _____

_____

_____

2. _____

_____

_____

3. _____

_____

_____

4. _____

_____

_____

5. _____

_____

_____

6. _____

_____

_____

7. _____

_____

_____

8. _____

_____

_____

9. _____

_____

_____

10. _____

_____

_____

E. (optional) Creative Writing

Use some or all of the words from the choice box to write one or more paragraphs or a short story on a separate piece of paper.

Lesson 16

PREFIX		ROOT		SUFFIX	
in-	in, into; not	**anim**	spirit, life	**it-able**	able to be
		cred	believe	**-ate**	to make, to act; one who, that which
		equ	equal, fair	**-ence**	state, quality, act
				-ible	able to be
				-ity	state, quality, act
				-ulous	having the quality of

A. Spelling and Defining Words

Write each word from the choice box next to its definition.

credible	equity	animate	credence
incredible	equitable	inanimate	credulous
incredulous	equanimity		

1. _____ to give spirit, life, motion, or activity to

2. _____ calm temperament; evenness of temper

3. _____ belief; acceptance as true or valid

4. _____ too extraordinary and impossible to believe

5. _____ disbelieving; not believing

6. _____ not filled with life or spirit; motionless

7. _____ able to be believed; believable; reliable

8. _____ believing too readily; gullible

9. _____ fairness; state of being just or fair

10. _____ fair; just

B. Completing the Sentence

Write the best word from the gray box to complete each sentence.

1. The tightrope walker performed the most _____ balancing act we had ever seen.

   incredible   credulous   credible

2. The student's excuse for tardiness received a/an _____ look from the teacher.

   credulous   equitable   incredulous

3. Brooke's _____ was apparent even when things got stressful.

   equanimity   equity   credence

4. The eyewitness gave _____ to the suspect's story.

   equity   credence   equanimity

5. The graphic artist's job was to _____ the cartoon characters.

   inanimate   credible   animate

6. Con artists thrive on cheating _____ people.

   credulous   incredulous   inanimate

7. The Supreme Court must judge each case with complete _____.

   equanimity   equity   credence

8. The lawsuit ended with an _____ settlement.

   incredulous   inanimate   equitable

9. The witness's testimony was deemed to be _____.

   credible   equitable   credulous

10. He stared in amazement at the _____ carvings of the presidents on Mount Rushmore.

    animate   inanimate   credulous

C. Defining the Word Parts

Write the definition from the choice box next to its correct word part. A definition may be used more than once.

> - believe
> - state, quality, act
> - able to be
> - in, into; not
> - to make, to act; one who, that which
>
> - spirit, life
> - an action or process
> - having the quality of
> - equal, fair
> - state, quality, act

1. -ence _____

2. equ _____

3. -ate _____

4. in- _____

5. cred _____

6. -ible _____

7. -ity _____

8. it-able _____

9. anim _____

10. -ulous _____

D. Writing Sentences

Use each word from the choice box to write a sentence in context so that its meaning is clear to the reader.

animate	credence	incredulous	credible	equity
equanimity	incredible	inanimate	credulous	equitable

1. _____

_____

_____

2. _____

_____

_____

3. _____

_____

_____

4. _____

_____

_____

5. _____

_____

_____

6. _____

_____

_____

7. _____

_____

_____

8. _____

_____

_____

9. _____

_____

_____

10. _____

_____

_____

E. (optional) Creative Writing

Use some or all of the words from the choice box to write one or more paragraphs or a short story on a separate piece of paper.

Review
Lessons 15 and 16

A. Write each word part from the choice box next to its definition.

-ary	fract/frag	-ile	-ure	equ	-ence	it-able
-al	-ation	-ion	anim	pre-	-ible	
in-	-ity/il-ity	-ment	cred	-ate	-ulous	

1. _____ in, into; not

2. _____ spirit, life

3. _____ to make, to act; one who, that which

4. _____ believe

5. _____ equal, fair

6. _____ state, quality, act

7. _____ able to be

8. _____ state, quality, act

9. _____ having the quality of

10. _____ that which; someone or something that belongs to; of, related to; one who

11. _____ like, of, relating to

12. _____ break

13. _____ an action or process; state, quality, act

14. _____ that which, state, quality, act

15. _____ state, quality, act; that which; process, condition

16. _____ like, related to; an action or process

17. _____ state, quality, act

18. _____ an action or process

19. _____ able to be

B. Write the letter of the correct definition for each word.

WORD		DEFINITION
1. fragility	_____	(a) not filled with life or spirit; motionless
2. fragmentary	_____	(b) able to be believed; believable; reliable
3. fractional	_____	(c) believing too readily; gullible
4. animate	_____	(d) fairness; the state of being just or fair
5. incredible	_____	(e) fair; just
6. fragmental	_____	(f) a part or element of a larger whole
7. incredulous	_____	(g) a break, crack, or split
8. credence	_____	(h) the act of breaking the limits or rules
9. equanimity	_____	(i) easily broken; delicate
10. fragmentation	_____	(j) a broken piece
11. equity	_____	(k) to give spirit, life, motion, or activity to
12. fragile	_____	(l) calm temperament; evenness of temper
13. infraction	_____	(m) belief; acceptance as true or valid
14. equitable	_____	(n) too extraordinary and impossible to believe
15. fracture	_____	(o) disbelieving; not believing
16. credulous	_____	(p) related to being very small; insignificant
17. inanimate	_____	(q) state of delicateness
18. fraction	_____	(r) related to being incomplete or broken
19. credible	_____	(s) not complete; disconnected
20. fragment	_____	(t) process of breaking, cracking, or splitting; that which is broken or divided

C. Use the jumbled letters to write the correct word for each definition.

JUMBLED LETTERS	DEFINITION	WORD
1. iaqbeteul	fair; just	_____
2. matneai	to give spirit, life, motion, or activity to	_____
3. atnygmrfrae	not complete; disconnected	_____
4. rctoanfi	a part or element of a larger whole	_____
5. scurudelo	believing too readily; gullible	_____
6. nqauyetiim	calm temperament; evenness of temper	_____
7. emngarnoftait	process of breaking, cracking, or splitting; that which is broken or divided	_____
8. uetcrrfa	a break, crack, or split	_____
9. tyique	fairness; the state of being just or fair	_____
10. necerdec	belief; acceptance as true or valid	_____
11. lagfrntmae	related to being incomplete or broken	_____
12. itnnafrcio	the act of breaking the limits or rules	_____
13. eelirbdc	able to be believed; believable; reliable	_____
14. itneminaa	not filled with life or spirit; motionless	_____
15. taifrilgy	state of delicateness	_____
16. otflraacin	related to being very small; insignificant	_____
17. igreafl	easily broken; delicate	_____
18. liedbreinc	too extraordinary and impossible to believe	_____
19. egfatmnr	a broken piece	_____
20. urlicsenuod	disbelieving; not believing	_____

D. Write the best word from the gray box to complete each sentence.

1. Jeremy would be a good treasurer for the club because of his _____.

   credence   infraction   equanimity

2. The owner of the smashed car was _____ that no one witnessed the

   accident on the busy street.

   incredulous   credulous   inanimate

3. The young man committed a driving _____ the week after he received his

   driver's license.

   fragmentation   infraction   fraction

4. A mere _____ of the members attended the conference.

   fragment   fraction   infraction

5. We agreed that they were asking a/an _____ price for the antiques.

   inanimate   credulous   equitable

6. When she fell, Bailey suffered a _____ of her wrist.

   fracture   fraction   fragment

7. A governing body should always make decisions based on the principle of

   _____.

   fragility   equity   equanimity

8. These glasses are much too _____ for everyday use.

   incredible   fragile   fragmental

9. The archaeologist discovered a _____ of the ancient pottery.

   fragment   fracture   fragmentation

10. We've heard _____ information about the severity of the earthquake.

   fractional   equitable   credible

D. (continued) Write the best word from the gray box to complete each sentence.

11. Since Skyler was very sheltered, she had a/an _____ view of life.

credulous   fragile   incredible

12. A/An _____ description of the person was sufficient for the artist to paint a portrait.

equitable   fragmental   fragile

13. The new software is just a/an _____ improvement over the old software.

incredulous   fragmentary   fractional

14. The ancient Egyptians worshipped _____ objects.

fragmental   inanimate   credible

15. It's good advice to not put much _____ in idle gossip.

credence   equity   fragmentation

16. Dad moved our family to another state because of a/an _____ job opportunity.

fractional   incredible   credulous

17. She gave us only a/an _____ account of the event.

fragile   incredulous   fragmentary

18. The teacher tried to _____ the bored students.

animate   inanimate   incredulous

19. Mom made the _____ of her crystal vases quite clear to the movers.

equanimity   fragility   infraction

20. The _____ of the famous statue was due to years of erosion.

fracture   infraction   fragmentation

Lesson 17

PREFIX	
ab-	away, from
bene-	good, well
de-	from, away, down, apart; not
in-	in, into; not

ROOT	
duct	lead
vol	will, wish

SUFFIX	
-ence	state, quality, act
-ent	one who, that which; like, related to
-ion	an action or process; state, quality, act
-ive	tending to or performing
i-tion	state, quality, act

A. Spelling and Defining Words

Write each word from the choice box next to its definition.

abduction	benevolent	benevolence	abduct
deduction	volition	induction	deductive
induct	deduct		

1. _____ to subtract; to take away

2. _____ to take away by force

3. _____ to formally install someone to an office or position

4. _____ showing kindness or goodwill

5. _____ the act of making a choice or a decision

6. _____ a subtraction of an amount

7. _____ the process of formally installing someone to an office or position

8. _____ the act of doing good; kindliness

9. _____ a taking away by force

10. _____ tending to use logic or reason to form a conclusion

B. Completing the Sentence
Write the best word from the gray box to complete each sentence.

1. The waiter made a/an _____ from the bill to make up for the customers'
    long wait for their food to arrive.

    volition   deduction   induction

2. Due to the wealthy man's _____, the hospital now has a new wing.

    benevolence   volition   abduction

3. In Greek mythology, the _____ of Helen from Sparta began the
    Trojan War.

    abduction   induction   deduction

4. The student's science report was based solely on _____ reasoning.

    benevolent   deductive   induction

5. The _____ doctor volunteered his services to the homeless.

    volition   benevolent   deductive

6. Dad said he would _____ the cost of the broken window from
    my allowance.

    induct   abduct   deduct

7. Next Friday morning we will have the registration and _____ of
    all draftees.

    induction   abduction   deduction

8. They failed at their attempt to _____ the victim for a ransom.

    induct   deduct   abduct

9. On Wednesday, the board members will _____ the new officers.

    deduct   abduct   induct

10. Bonita joined the Peace Corps of her own _____.

    deduction   benevolence   volition

C. Defining the Word Parts
Write the definition from the choice box next to its correct word part. A definition may be used more than once.

- away, from
- lead
- one who, that which; like, related to
- good, well
- from, away, down, apart; not
- before, in front of

- in, into; not
- will, wish
- an action or process; state, quality, act
- state, quality, act
- tending to or performing

---

1. -ive _____

2. in- _____

3. duct _____

4. -ent _____

5. -ion _____

6. ab- _____

7. bene- _____

8. vol _____

9. i-tion _____

10. de- _____

11. -ence _____

D. Writing Sentences

Use each word from the choice box to write a sentence in context so that its meaning is clear to the reader.

abduction	induct	volition	benevolence	abduct
deduction	benevolent	deduct	induction	deductive

1. _____

_____

_____

2. _____

_____

_____

3. _____

_____

_____

4. _____

_____

_____

5. _____

_____

_____

6. _____

_____

_____

7. _____

_____

_____

8. _____

_____

_____

9. _____

_____

_____

10. _____

_____

_____

E. (optional) Creative Writing

Use some or all of the words from the choice box to write one or more paragraphs or a short story on a separate piece of paper.

Lesson 18

PREFIX		ROOT		SUFFIX	
a-	away, from; not, without	vers/ verse/ vert	turn	-ion	an action or process; state, quality, act
con-	with, together				
extro-	outside of				
in-	in, into; not				
intro-	within				
tra-	across, through				

A. Spelling and Defining Words

Write each word from the choice box next to its definition.

aversion	introversion	avert	extroversion
convert	traverse	conversion	invert
extrovert	introvert		

1. _____ to move across or turn back and forth across

2. _____ an outgoing person

3. _____ turning inward; focusing on oneself

4. _____ to turn into or transform

5. _____ the act of turning away from; a dislike of something

6. _____ a person whose interest is more in himself than in others

7. _____ to turn away; to keep from happening

8. _____ a change from one thing, state, or religion to another

9. _____ turning outward; focusing on others

10. _____ to turn inside out or upside down

B. Completing the Sentence
Write the best word from the gray box to complete each sentence.

1. Native American tribes would _____ the plains in search of buffalo.

    avert   traverse   convert

2. No one was surprised when Blake, who was a/an _____, grew up to be a famous comedian.

    extrovert   introvert   convert

3. Vegetarians have an _____ to eating meat.

    introversion   aversion   conversion

4. Nora planned to _____ the garage into another bedroom.

    traverse   avert   convert

5. Gavin believed his _____ came from being an only child.

    introversion   aversion   conversion

6. An _____ tends to spend much of the time alone.

    extrovert   introvert   aversion

7. Scarlett tried to _____ her head so we couldn't see her face.

    avert   convert   traverse

8. The _____ of a caterpillar into a butterfly is miraculous.

    aversion   extroversion   conversion

9. Maria's _____ makes her the life of the party.

    aversion   extroversion   introversion

10. If you _____ the nine, it will look like a six.

    invert   convert   avert

C. Defining the Word Parts

Write the definition from the choice box next to its correct word part.

> • away, from; not, without
> • with, together
> • to do, to drive
> • within
> • across, through
>
> • turn
> • an action or process; state, quality, act
> • in, into; not
> • outside of

1. tra-　　　_____

2. in-　　　_____

3. -ion　　　_____

4. intro-　　_____

5. con-　　　_____

6. vers/verse/vert　_____

7. a-　　　_____

8. extro-　　_____

D. Writing Sentences

Use each word from the choice box to write a sentence in context so that its meaning is clear to the reader.

aversion	extrovert	traverse	avert	extroversion
convert	introversion	introvert	conversion	invert

1. _____

    _____

    _____

2. _____

    _____

    _____

3. _____

    _____

    _____

4. _____

    _____

    _____

5. _____

    _____

    _____

6. _____

    _____

    _____

7. _____

    _____

    _____

8. _____

    _____

    _____

9. _____

    _____

    _____

10. _____

    _____

    _____

E. (optional) Creative Writing

Use some or all of the words from the choice box to write one or more paragraphs or a short story on a separate piece of paper.

Review
Lessons 17 and 18

A. Write each word part from the choice box next to its definition.

duct	in-	bene-	i-tion	-ive	intro-
ab-	vers/verse/vert	vol	-ate	a-	tra-
-ent	-ion	de-	-ence	con-	extro-

1. _____ with, together

2. _____ within

3. _____ away, from

4. _____ lead

5. _____ one who, that which; like, related to

6. _____ good, well

7. _____ from, away, down, apart; not

8. _____ away, from; not, without

9. _____ will, wish

10. _____ an action or process; state, quality, act

11. _____ state, quality, act

12. _____ tending to or performing

13. _____ state, quality, act

14. _____ outside of

15. _____ turn

16. _____ in, into; not

17. _____ across, through

B. Write the letter of the correct definition for each word.

WORD	DEFINITION

WORD

DEFINITION

1. induct _____

2. volition _____

3. traverse _____

4. convert _____

5. extrovert _____

6. aversion _____

7. abduction _____

8. benevolent _____

9. deduction _____

10. introversion _____

11. deduct _____

12. avert _____

13. conversion _____

14. extroversion _____

15. induction _____

16. abduct _____

17. deductive _____

18. invert _____

19. benevolence _____

20. introvert _____

(a) to subtract; to take away

(b) the process of formally installing someone to an office or position

(c) to take away by force

(d) the act of doing good; kindliness

(e) tending to use logic or reason to form a conclusion

(f) a person whose interest is more in himself than in others

(g) to turn away; to keep from happening

(h) a change from one thing, state, or religion to another

(i) turning outward; focusing on others

(j) to turn inside out or upside down

(k) to formally install someone to an office or position

(l) a taking away by force

(m) showing kindness or goodwill

(n) a subtraction of an amount

(o) the act of making a choice or a decision

(p) to move across or turn back and forth across

(q) an outgoing person

(r) turning inward; focusing on oneself

(s) to turn into or transform

(t) the act of turning away from; a dislike of something

C. Use the jumbled letters to write the correct word for each definition.

JUMBLED LETTERS	DEFINITION	WORD
1. arvosein	the act of turning away from; a dislike of something	_____
2. tnvire	to turn inside out or upside down	_____
3. uoctabind	a taking away by force	_____
4. dueidcetv	tending to use logic or reason to form a conclusion	_____
5. vrotcen	to turn into or transform	_____
6. rtneioosxevr	turning outward; focusing on others	_____
7. ctndui	to formally install someone to an office or position	_____
8. lnbenecoeve	the act of doing good; kindliness	_____
9. ovxerttre	an outgoing person	_____
10. coseionvnr	a change from one thing, state, or religion to another	_____
11. eeeotbnlnv	showing kindness or goodwill	_____
12. acbdut	to take away by force	_____
13. trnirisonevo	turning inward; focusing on oneself	_____
14. atrve	to turn away; to keep from happening	_____
15. volnioit	the act of making a choice or a decision	_____
16. icnduinot	the process of formally installing someone to an office or position	_____
17. cdetdu	to subtract; to take away	_____
18. rvareset	to move across or turn back and forth across	_____
19. rtenriotv	a person whose interest is more in himself than in others	_____
20. odtceduin	a subtraction of an amount	_____

D. Write the best word from the gray box to complete each sentence.

1. Lucy was voted most likely to succeed because of her outgoing and

   _____ personality.   (deductive benevolent introversion)

2. A/An _____ of points would be taken if a music academy student did not

   practice daily.   (deduction conversion induction)

3. Jake cleaned his room of his own _____, instead of waiting to be told to

   do so.   (volition aversion benevolence)

4. During a game, a soccer player will _____ the field many times.

   (avert traverse convert)

5. The bank will _____ the monthly fee from my account.

   (abduct induct deduct)

6. The _____ of the new officers will take place at a private ceremony.

   (conversion induction abduction)

7. Jim is an _____ who loves to meet people.

   (extrovert introvert avert)

8. We watched the magician _____ the hat to prove it was empty.

   (abduct convert invert)

9. An example of _____ reasoning is that whenever you add three plus five

   together you will always get eight.   (benevolent deductive conversion)

10. A thief might try to _____ an expensive breed of dog if given the

    opportunity.   (abduct induct deduct)

11. The playground attendant smiled with _____ at the noisy children.

> aversion   benevolence   volition

12. The firemen hoped to _____ a major fire by arriving speedily.

> invert   traverse   avert

13. I have a strong _____ to spicy foods.

> volition   aversion   extroversion

14. It was interesting to see how they _____ various grains into flour.

> avert   invert   convert

15. The report of an _____ by aliens was totally discredited.

> abduction   induction   aversion

16. The girl's _____ escalated after she lost her mother.

> aversion   conversion   introversion

17. The team will _____ two new members next year.

> abduct   avert   induct

18. The _____ from electric to gas heat will be very cost effective.

> extroversion   conversion   induction

19. Kyle was too much of an _____ to run for class president.

> introvert   aversion   extrovert

20. Juanita's extreme _____ was causing problems with co-workers.

> benevolence   aversion   extroversion

Lesson 19

PREFIX		ROOT		SUFFIX	
e-	out, away, from	**loqu**	speak	**-acious**	having the quality of
mis-	bad, wrong	**nom/** **nomin**	name, law, custom, order	**-al**	like, related to; an action or process
				-ation	an action or process
				-ence	state, quality, act
				-ent	one who, that which; like, related to
				-er	one who, that which
				-ly	in the manner of; having the quality of
				-ness	state, quality, act

A. Spelling and Defining Words

Write each word from the choice box next to its definition.

> eloquent   misnomer   nominally   loquaciousness
> loquacious   nomination   eloquently   loquaciously
> nominal   eloquence

1. _____   very talkative

2. _____   an error in naming a person or thing

3. _____   being something in name only but not in reality

4. _____   in a very talkative or wordy manner

5. _____   speaking beautifully and forcefully

6. _____   action of choosing someone for a position, office, etc.

7. _____   speech that is vivid, fluent, forceful, and graceful

8. _____   in name only; in a very small amount

9. _____   the quality of being very talkative

10. _____   speaking in a vivid, fluent, forceful, and graceful manner

B. Completing the Sentence

Write the best word from the gray box to complete each sentence.

1. Sadie acted out the skit both energetically and _____.

    nominally loquaciously nominal

2. The teacher corrected the student's _____ in his report.

    misnomer eloquence loquaciousness

3. Until the official election, David was designated the _____ leader.

    eloquent loquacious nominal

4. The young princess impressed people with her _____ address to the peace organization.

    nominal loquacious eloquent

5. The new neighbors proved to be friendly and _____.

    nominally eloquent loquacious

6. As a talk show host, Asher's _____ serves him well.

    eloquence loquaciousness misnomer

7. The senator was only _____ elected to office.

    nominally loquaciously eloquently

8. He won the _____ by a landslide.

    misnomer eloquence nomination

9. Some say I have the gift of gab, but I prefer to call it _____.

    eloquence misnomer nomination

10. Chloe's acceptance speech was brief but _____ delivered.

    nominally eloquently loquaciously

C. Defining the Word Parts

Write the definition from the choice box next to its correct word part. A definition may be used more than once.

> - out, away, from
> - bad, wrong
> - with, together
> - speak
> - name, law, custom, order
> - having the quality of
>
> - like, related to; an action or process
> - state, quality, act
> - one who, that which; like, related to
> - one who, that which
> - an action or process
> - in the manner of; having the quality of

1. -ation   _____

2. e-   _____

3. loqu   _____

4. -ly   _____

5. -acious   _____

6. -ence   _____

7. nom/nomin   _____

8. mis-   _____

9. -al   _____

10. -ness   _____

11. -er   _____

12. -ent   _____

D. Writing Sentences

Use each word from the choice box to write a sentence in context so that its meaning is clear to the reader.

eloquent	nominal	nomination	nominally	loquaciousness
loquacious	misnomer	eloquence	eloquently	loquaciously

1. _____

   _____

   _____

2. _____

   _____

   _____

3. _____

   _____

   _____

4. _____

   _____

   _____

5. _____

   _____

   _____

6. _____

   _____

   _____

7. _____

   _____

   _____

8. _____

   _____

   _____

9. _____

   _____

   _____

10. _____

   _____

   _____

E. (optional) Creative Writing

Use some or all of the words from the choice box to write one or more paragraphs or a short story on a separate piece of paper.

Lesson 20

PREFIX	
de-	from, away, down, apart; not
in-	in, into; not

ROOT	
carni	flesh, meat
manu	hand
scrib/ scribe/ script	write, written
vor/ vour	eat

SUFFIX	
-able	able to be
-acious	having the quality of
-al	like, related to; an action or process
-ion	an action or process; state, quality, act
-ous	having the quality of

A. Spelling and Defining Words

Write each word from the choice box next to its definition.

> manual   devour   inscription   description
> manuscript   voracious   inscribe   indescribable
> carnivorous   describe

1. _____ flesh-eating

2. _____ desiring or eating food in great quantities

3. _____ having to do with the hands

4. _____ to eat quickly

5. _____ a handwritten document or author's original text

6. _____ to represent with words or pictures

7. _____ action or process of picturing in words

8. _____ to write or engrave on some surface

9. _____ not able to be described

10. _____ an engraving on a coin or other object

B. Completing the Sentence
Write the best word from the gray box to complete each sentence.

1. After being stranded in the wilderness for three days, Jordyn had a
   _____ appetite.

   carnivorous   voracious   manual

2. Alex liked his job as a landscaper because it involved _____ labor and
   being outside.

   manual   indescribable   voracious

3. Lions and tigers are _____ animals.

   indescribable   manual   carnivorous

4. My dog will _____ her food as soon as the dish hits the floor.

   devour   inscribe   describe

5. Reading an ancient _____ can reveal information about a culture that no
   longer exists.

   description   inscription   manuscript

6. Ross tried very hard to _____ the car that ran into his bike.

   inscribe   describe   devour

7. The _____ on the medallion was very meaningful.

   inscription   manuscript   description

8. The artistry of Michelangelo's *Pieta* is _____.

   voracious   carnivorous   indescribable

9. She gave an accurate _____ of the robber's appearance.

   description   inscription   manuscript

10. Bill had the jeweler _____ their wedding date on the lovely locket he
    bought for his wife.

    describe   inscribe   devour

C. Defining the Word Parts

Write the definition from the choice box next to its correct word part. A definition may be used more than once.

> - from, away, down, apart; not
> - flesh, meat
> - hand
> - write, written
> - eat
> - take, hold
> - having the quality of
> - like, related to; an action or process
> - in, into; not
> - able to be
> - an action or process; state, quality, act

1. vor/vour   _____

2. -able   _____

3. de-   _____

4. -acious   _____

5. carni   _____

6. in-   _____

7. -al   _____

8. -ous   _____

9. scrib/scribe/
    script   _____

10. manu   _____

11. -ion   _____

D. Writing Sentences

Use each word from the choice box to write a sentence in context so that its meaning is clear to the reader.

manual	carnivorous	voracious	inscription	description
manuscript	devour	describe	inscribe	indescribable

1. _____

_____

_____

2. _____

_____

_____

3. _____

_____

_____

4. _____

_____

_____

5. _____

_____

_____

6. _____

_____

_____

7. _____

_____

_____

8. _____

_____

_____

9. _____

_____

_____

10. _____

_____

_____

E. (optional) Creative Writing

Use some or all of the words from the choice box to write one or more paragraphs or a short story on a separate piece of paper.

Review
Lessons 19 and 20

A. Write each word part from the choice box next to its definition.

de-	-ation	-ence	-al	-er	-ure
-ion	loqu	-ness	-ent	manu	vor/vour
in-	e-	-ly	nom/nomin	-able	-ous
carni	mis-	-acious	scrib/scribe/script		

1. _____ from, away, down, apart; not

2. _____ flesh, meat

3. _____ hand

4. _____ write, written

5. _____ out, away, from

6. _____ bad, wrong

7. _____ speak

8. _____ name, law, custom, order

9. _____ having the quality of

10. _____ like, related to; an action or process

11. _____ state, quality, act

12. _____ one who, that which; like, related to

13. _____ one who, that which

14. _____ an action or process

15. _____ in the manner of; having the quality of

16. _____ state, quality, act

17. _____ eat

18. _____ having the quality of

19. _____ in, into; not

20. _____ able to be

21. _____ an action or process; state, quality, act

B. Write the letter of the correct definition for each word.

WORD		DEFINITION
1. manual _____	(a)	very talkative
2. eloquent _____	(b)	an error in naming a person or thing
3. manuscript _____	(c)	being something in name only but not in reality
4. devour _____	(d)	in a very talkative or wordy manner
5. eloquently _____	(e)	to represent with words or pictures
6. eloquence _____	(f)	action or process of picturing in words
7. carnivorous _____	(g)	to write or engrave on some surface
8. nomination _____	(h)	not able to be described
9. loquaciousness _____	(i)	an engraving on a coin or other object
10. inscribe _____	(j)	flesh-eating
11. nominally _____	(k)	desiring or eating food in great quantities
12. loquacious _____	(l)	having to do with the hands
13. loquaciously _____	(m)	to eat quickly; to enjoy avidly
14. nominal _____	(n)	a handwritten document or author's original text
15. misnomer _____	(o)	speaking beautifully and forcefully
16. indescribable _____	(p)	action of choosing someone for a position, office, etc.
17. description _____	(q)	speech that is vivid, fluent, forceful, and graceful
18. voracious _____	(r)	in name only; in a very small amount
19. inscription _____	(s)	the quality of being very talkative
20. describe _____	(t)	speaking in a vivid, fluent, forceful, and graceful manner

C. Use the jumbled letters to write the correct word for each definition.

JUMBLED LETTERS	DEFINITION	WORD
1. nualam	having to do with the hands	_____
2. breiibescldna	not able to be described	_____
3. ltnqeeou	speaking beautifully and forcefully	_____
4. mialnlyon	in name only; in a very small amount	_____
5. amrpunctsi	a handwritten document or author's original text	_____
6. bnscerii	to write or engrave on some surface	_____
7. mnonail	being something in name only but not in reality	_____
8. cyquaoiluosl	in a very talkative or wordy manner	_____
9. rsincuraovo	flesh-eating	_____
10. iiorpcsnnit	an engraving on a coin or other object	_____
11. mnmisoer	an error in naming a person or thing	_____
12. omantniion	action of choosing someone for a position, office, etc.	_____
13. qelencueo	speech that is vivid, fluent, forceful, and graceful	_____
14. ssqsocueioulan	the quality of being very talkative	_____
15. ourved	to eat quickly	_____
16. esdercib	to represent with words or pictures	_____
17. cuoaoirvs	desiring or eating food in great quantities	_____
18. eorntcpiisd	action or process of picturing in words	_____
19. lqtonueely	speaking in a vivid, fluent, forceful, and graceful manner	_____
20. qaulcosoui	very talkative	_____

D. Write the best word from the gray box to complete each sentence.

1. The little girl surprised everyone with her _____ appetite.

   loquacious   voracious   eloquent

2. The announcer humorously and _____ introduced the new comedian.

   eloquent   nominally   loquaciously

3. Naming a horse Lightning after it lost six consecutive races is a huge _____.

   misnomer   description   manuscript

4. They tried to _____ their journey in vivid detail.

   inscribe   describe   nominal

5. The defense attorney made a/an _____ plea for his client's acquittal.

   voracious   nominal   eloquent

6. Membership in the club is by _____ only.

   nomination   inscription   description

7. They plan to _____ the monument with each soldier's name.

   devour   inscribe   describe

8. The show featured dogs of every _____.

   inscription   nomination   description

9. Tyler was paid _____ for his hard work.

   nominally   eloquently   loquaciously

10. The view of the Grand Canyon is _____.

   nominal   indescribable   voracious

D. (continued) Write the best word from the gray box to complete each sentence.

11. Helen is so _____ I can't get a word in edgewise.

        carnivorous eloquent loquacious

12. The president of the company had just a/an _____ position.

        manual indescribable nominal

13. They chose someone who could _____ announce the awards.

        eloquently nominally loquaciously

14. The sports car has a _____ transmission.

        nominal manual loquacious

15. Joaquin showed me the _____ of his new play.

        manuscript misnomer description

16. After the hike, George felt so hungry that he could not wait to _____
        his food.

        describe inscribe devour

17. The excessive _____ of the candidate annoyed the voters.

        inscription loquaciousness eloquence

18. He spoke with dignity and _____ on the need for policy reform.

        eloquence loquaciousness nomination

19. The _____ on the ancient tombstone was barely legible.

        manuscript description inscription

20. My science report was about the _____ hunting spiders.

        indescribable carnivorous eloquent

Lesson 21

PREFIX	
bi-	two
cent-	hundred
per-	through, very
uni-	one

ROOT	
annu/ enni	year
later	side

SUFFIX	
-al	like, related to; an action or process
-ly	in the manner of; having the quality of

A. Spelling and Defining Words

Write each word from the choice box next to its definition.

> bicentennial   bilateral   laterally   annually
> centennial   unilateral   annual   biannual
> perennial   lateral

1. _____   affecting one side of something

2. _____   of, or relating to an age or period of 200 years

3. _____   of, or involving two sides; reciprocal

4. _____   of, or relating to an age or period of 100 years

5. _____   lasting through many years

6. _____   of, or relating to the side

7. _____   related to a period of one year

8. _____   happening twice a year

9. _____   by, to, or from the side; sideways

10. _____   in the manner of occurring once a year

B. Completing the Sentence
Write the best word from the gray box to complete each sentence.

1. Each spring the _____ flowers she planted during her first year at the

    house bloom again.

    annual   perennial   biannual

2. In 1976, the United States had its _____ anniversary.

    bicentennial   centennial   perennial

3. The United States and Mexico benefit from a _____ trade agreement.

    unilateral   lateral   bilateral

4. The country made a _____ decision to stop selling arms.

    bilateral   unilateral   lateral

5. The _____ celebration honored the author John Steinbeck, who was born

    in the early 1900s.

    centennial   perennial   unilateral

6. From a _____ view you can see the mountain's steep incline.

    bilateral   biannual   lateral

7. My credit card company charges a/an _____ fee of $50.00.

    annual   perennial   unilateral

8. The fierce wind blew the tumbleweed _____ across the open field.

    annually   laterally   perennial

9. The arts and craft show is a/an _____ event in December and June.

    biannual   annual   perennial

10. Our family reunion is held _____ in August.

    bilateral   annually   laterally

C. Defining the Word Parts

Write the definition from the choice box next to its correct word part.

> - two
> - side
> - in the manner of; having the quality of
> - hundred
> - year
>
> - through, very
> - apart, aside
> - like, related to; an action or process
> - one

1. -al   _____

2. cent-   _____

3. later   _____

4. bi-   _____

5. -ly   _____

6. uni-   _____

7. per-   _____

8. annu/enni   _____

D. Writing Sentences

Use each word from the choice box to write a sentence in context so that its meaning is clear to the reader.

bicentennial	perennial	unilateral	laterally	annually
centennial	bilateral	lateral	annual	biannual

1. _____

_____

_____

2. _____

_____

_____

3. _____

_____

_____

4. _____

_____

_____

5. _____

_____

_____

6. _____

_____

_____

7. _____

_____

_____

8. _____

_____

_____

9. _____

_____

_____

10. _____

_____

_____

E. (optional) Creative Writing

Use some or all of the words from the choice box to write one or more paragraphs or a short story on a separate piece of paper.

Lesson 22

PREFIX		ROOT		SUFFIX	
con-	with, together	tempor	time	it-able	able to be
ex-	out, away from	ver	truth	-acious	having the quality of
				-acity	the quality of
				-al	like, related to; an action or process
				-aneous	having the quality of
				-ary	that which; someone or something that belongs to; of, related to; one who
				ific-ation	an action or process
				-ly	in the manner of; having the quality of

A. Spelling and Defining Words

Write each word from the choice box next to its definition.

> contemporary   temporal   veracious   extemporaneously
> temporary   veritable   verification   contemporaneously
> veracity   extemporaneous

1. _____   lasting for a limited time

2. _____   of the same time; modern time

3. _____   done without any preparation; impromptu

4. _____   truth; honesty

5. _____   of, or related to a limited time as opposed to eternity; temporary

6. _____   having the quality of existing, occurring, or originating at the same time

7. _____   being in fact the true or real thing; actual

8. _____   the process of confirming the truth

9. _____   in a spur of the moment manner

10. _____   having the quality of being honest; truthful

B. Completing the Sentence

Write the best word from the gray box to complete each sentence.

1. The mayor was known for his _____ speaking ability.

   temporary   extemporaneous   veritable

2. Although the mother was upset with her son, she praised him for his _____ after he admitted to eating all of the candy.

   veracity   veracious   verification

3. The Dalai Lama is the spiritual and _____ leader of the Tibetan people.

   contemporary   extemporaneous   temporal

4. Bad weather caused a _____ delay in their plans.

   temporary   temporal   contemporary

5. He enjoyed both _____ and classical music.

   extemporaneous   temporary   contemporary

6. The wedding reception was a/an _____ feast.

   temporal   veritable   extemporaneous

7. The two controversial books were _____ published.

   contemporaneously   extemporaneously   contemporary

8. Several witnesses provided sufficient _____ of his alibi.

   veritable   veracity   verification

9. Our professor is known for giving quizzes _____.

   extemporaneously   contemporary   contemporaneously

10. Ben is trusted by everyone because he has a reputation for being _____.

    temporal   veracious   extemporaneous

C. Defining the Word Parts

Write the definition from the choice box next to its correct word part. A definition may be used more than once.

> * back, again
> * with, together
> * out, away, from
> * truth
> * the quality of
> * time
> * an action or process
>
> * having the quality of
> * that which; someone or something that belongs to; of, related to; one who
> * like, related to; an action or process
> * able to be
> * in the manner of; having the quality of

1. tempor _____

2. it-able _____

3. -acity _____

4. con- _____

5. -al _____

6. ver _____

7. -ly _____

8. ific-ation _____

9. ex- _____

10. -aneous _____

11. -ary _____

12. -acious _____

D. Writing Sentences

Use each word from the choice box to write a sentence in context so that its meaning is clear to the reader.

contemporary	temporary	temporal	veracious	extemporaneously
contemporaneous	veracity	veritable	verification	contemporaneously

1. _____

2. _____

3. _____

4. _____

5. _____

6. _____

7. _____

8. _____

9. _____

10. _____

E. (optional) Creative Writing

Use some or all of the words from the choice box to write one or more paragraphs or a short story on a separate piece of paper.

Review
Lessons 21 and 22

A. Write each word part from the choice box next to its definition.

-ly	memor	ex-	it-able	-aneous	per-	-al
ver	con-	-acity	cent-	ific-ation	bi-	uni-
tempor	-acious	-ary	later	annu/enni		

1. _____ two

2. _____ hundred

3. _____ in the manner of; having the quality of

4. _____ able to be

5. _____ through, very

6. _____ one

7. _____ year

8. _____ having the quality of

9. _____ side

10. _____ like, related to; an action or process

11. _____ with, together

12. _____ out, away, from

13. _____ an action or process

14. _____ time

15. _____ truth

16. _____ the quality of

17. _____ having the quality of

18. _____ that which; someone or something that belongs to; of, related to; one who

B. Write the letter of the correct definition for each word.

WORD		DEFINITION
1. annual	_____	(a) lasting for a limited time
2. perennial	_____	(b) of the same time; modern time
3. veracious	_____	(c) done without any preparation; impromptu
4. contemporaneously	_____	(d) truth; honesty
5. bilateral	_____	(e) of, or related to a limited time as opposed to eternity; temporary
6. extemporaneously	_____	(f) of, or relating to the side
7. temporary	_____	(g) related to a period of one year
8. bicentennial	_____	(h) happening twice a year
9. centennial	_____	(i) by, to, or from the side; sideways
10. unilateral	_____	(j) in the manner of occurring once a year
11. veracity	_____	(k) having the quality of existing, occurring, or originating at the same time
12. verification	_____	(l) being in fact the true or real thing; actual
13. veritable	_____	(m) the process of confirming the truth
14. lateral	_____	(n) in a spur of the moment manner
15. extemporaneous	_____	(o) having the quality of being honest; truthful
16. annually	_____	(p) affecting one side of something
17. biannual	_____	(q) of, or relating to an age or period of 200 years
18. temporal	_____	(r) of, or involving two sides; reciprocal
19. laterally	_____	(s) of, or relating to an age or period of 100 years
20. contemporary	_____	(t) lasting through many years

C. Use the jumbled letters to write the correct word for each definition.

JUMBLED LETTERS	DEFINITION	WORD
1. tcorniiefvia	the process of confirming the truth	_____
2. prrcaomenoyt	of, the same time; modern time	_____
3. nynallau	in the manner of occurring once a year	_____
4. bcnteneilian	of, or relating to an age or period of 200 years	_____
5. suaerociv	having the quality of being honest; truthful	_____
6. nrmteesuoepoxa	in a spur of the moment manner	_____
7. naalbuin	happening twice a year	_____
8. nencnitael	of, or relating to an age or period of 100 years	_____
9. sauepxrtmenoyole	done without any preparation; impromptu	_____
10. pomtarrye	lasting for a limited time	_____
11. aytaelrll	by, to, or from the side; sideways	_____
12. ianelpenr	lasting through many years	_____
13. ounamyereospoclnt	having the quality of existing, occurring, or originating at the same time	_____
14. traceviy	truth; honesty	_____
15. uananl	related to a period of one year	_____
16. ltearblai	of, or involving two sides; reciprocal	_____
17. emlpoart	of, or related to a limited time as opposed to eternity; temporary	_____
18. baievlret	being in fact the true or real thing; actual	_____
19. lltrauaien	affecting one side of something	_____
20. raatlel	of, or relating to the side	_____

D. Write the best word from the gray box to complete each sentence.

1. Having lived for ten decades, the grandmother was honored with a _____

   celebration.   perennial   centennial   bicentennial

2. Workers knew that the sandbags were only a _____ solution to stopping

   the flood water.   contemporary   temporary   unilateral

3. The elderly professor is a _____ gold mine of information.

                                        veritable   lateral   perennial

4. We trimmed the _____ branches of the tree.

                                        temporal   centennial   lateral

5. Our basement is cleaned out _____ whether it needs it or not.

                                    annually   laterally   extemporaneously

6. Amadeus Mozart and Antonio Salieri composed music _____.

                                extemporaneously   contemporaneously   annually

7. When the young man entered the monastery, he knew he would be giving up the

   _____ things in life.   temporal   veritable   perennial

8. The court required _____ that proved he was the owner of the property.

                                    veritable   veracity   verification

9. Unlike an airplane, a helicopter can move _____ in the air.

                                    laterally   annually   extemporaneously

10. I make _____ visits to my dentist.

                                     perennial   bilateral   biannual

11. The jury doubted the _____ of the felon.

> verification   veracity   veritable

12. Our _____ rainfall is about nine inches.

> annual   centennial   temporal

13. I was taken by surprise when asked to speak _____.

> annually   extemporaneously   contemporaneously

14. The book gives a _____ account of historical events.

> unilateral   temporal   veracious

15. Adding a scarf to her outfit gave it a _____ look.

> temporary   contemporary   veritable

16. Our garden is filled with both annual and _____ flowers.

> centennial   bicentennial   perennial

17. The workers protested because the owner made a _____ decision to shut down the factory.

> bilateral   veritable   unilateral

18. The famous poet recited a/an _____ piece of verse.

> extemporaneous   veracious   temporal

19. The _____ bustle had little to do with the historical events that occurred two centuries ago.

> centennial   bicentennial   perennial

20. The leaders of the two nations signed a/an _____ peace treaty.

> lateral   extemporaneous   bilateral

Lesson 23

PREFIX	
con-	with, together
en-	in, into
re-	back, again

ROOT	
dur/ dure	harden, to last, lasting
viv/ vive	live, life

SUFFIX	
-able	able to be
-acious	having the quality of
-al/ i-al	like, related to; an action or process
-ation	an action or process
-id	like, related to
-ly	in the manner of; having the quality of

A. Spelling and Defining Words

Write each word from the choice box next to its definition.

> durable   duration   endure   convivial
> vivid   vivacious   vividly   vivaciously
> revival   revive

1. _____ to remain, to last

2. _____ lively in appearance; bright; intense; strong

3. _____ to bring back to life or consciousness

4. _____ high-spirited and full of life

5. _____ having the quality of lasting

6. _____ lively, jovial, friendly

7. _____ in a bright or intense manner

8. _____ the act of bringing back to life; renewed interest in

9. _____ the length of time something lasts

10. _____ done in a high-spirited manner

B. Completing the Sentence
Write the best word from the gray box to complete each sentence.

1. The artist's use of _____ shapes and colors made his work
    very appealing.
    > durable   vivid   convivial

2. Denim is known for its _____ nature.
    > convivial   vivid   durable

3. Adalyn's hiccups lasted the _____ of the lunch hour.
    > durable   duration   revival

4. The _____ of the Broadway play proved to be a box office hit.
    > convivial   duration   revival

5. The actress performed her part so _____.
    > vividly   revival   vivaciously

6. Lucas described the event so _____ we believed it actually happened.
    > vivid   vividly   vivaciously

7. They used smelling salts to _____ the girl.
    > revival   endure   revive

8. The actress was loved by all because of her _____ personality.
    > vivacious   vivid   durable

9. They vowed that their love would _____ forever.
    > duration   endure   revive

10. It's fun to take a tour with _____ people.
    > durable   convivial   vivid

C. Defining the Word Parts
Write the definition from the choice box next to its correct word part.

> • with, together
> • able to be
> • live, life
> • back, again
> • truth
> • having the quality of
>
> • harden, to last, lasting
> • like, related to
> • an action or process
> • in the manner of, having the quality of
> • like, related to; an action or process
> • in, into

1. viv/vive   _____

2. -ly   _____

3. con-   _____

4. -able   _____

5. re-   _____

6. dur/dure   _____

7. -acious   _____

8. -id   _____

9. -al/ i-al   _____

10. -ation   _____

11. en-   _____

D. Writing Sentences

Use each word from the choice box to write a sentence in context so that its meaning is clear to the reader.

durable	revival	vivacious	endure	convivial
vivid	duration	revive	vividly	vivaciously

1. _____

   _____

   _____

2. _____

   _____

   _____

3. _____

   _____

   _____

4. _____

   _____

   _____

5. _____

   _____

   _____

6. _____

   _____

   _____

7. _____

   _____

   _____

8. _____

   _____

   _____

9. _____

   _____

   _____

10. _____

   _____

   _____

E. (optional) Creative Writing

Use some or all of the words from the choice box to write one or more paragraphs or a short story on a separate piece of paper.

Lesson 24

PREFIX	
ex-	out, away, from
pro-	for, before, forward

ROOT	
claim/ clam	call out, shout
equ/ equi*	equal, fair
voc	voice, call

SUFFIX	
-al	like, related to; an action or process
-ate	to make, to act; one who, that which
-ation	an action or process
-ity	state, quality, act
-ize	to make, to act

*For more information on connecting forms and combining vowels, please see page v in the Introduction.

A. Spelling and Defining Words

Write each word from the choice box next to its definition.

exclaim	equity	vocalize	proclaim
proclamation	equivocate	equate	vocation
equation	exclamation		

1. _____ to make, treat, or regard as equal or equivalent

2. _____ to cry out or speak in a strong or sudden manner

3. _____ to put into words, to utter, to speak

4. _____ fairness; the state of being just or fair

5. _____ to use misleading language that could be interpreted in different ways

6. _____ a statement of equality

7. _____ calling, profession, career

8. _____ to announce, to declare, to make public

9. _____ an outcry, a shout

10. _____ something announced officially in public

B. Completing the Sentence
Write the best word from the gray box to complete each sentence.

1. The skaters complained about the lack of _____ in the judges' decision.

    equity   equation   exclamation

2. The king issued a/an _____ that all foreign prisoners would be released
    and returned to their home countries.

    exclamation   equation   proclamation

3. The boss no longer believed the employee, because he continued to
    _____ about why he was late.

    proclaim   exclaim   equivocate

4. We heard the salesman _____ that his product would cure all ills.

    exclaim   equate   proclaim

5. Jean was a shy child who surprised her classmates when she jumped up to
    _____ that she thought the rules of the game were not fair.

    equate   exclaim   equivocate

6. Many people _____ wisdom with old age.

    equivocate   proclaim   equate

7. With a/an _____ of surprise she recognized her long-lost cousin.

    exclamation   proclamation   vocation

8. The _____ showed that two apples weighed the same as one melon.

    equation   vocation   exclamation

9. It would be better if you _____ your fears rather than suppress them.

    vocalize   equivocate   equate

10. Nursing is a very satisfying _____.

    exclamation   vocation   equation

C. Defining the Word Parts

Write the definition from the choice box next to its correct word part.

- to, toward, near
- to make, to act; one who, that which
- voice, call
- out, away, from
- an action or process
- state, quality, act
- call out, shout
- for, before, forward
- to make, to act
- equal, fair
- like, related to; an action or process

1. -ize   _____

2. ex-   _____

3. voc   _____

4. pro-   _____

5. claim/clam   _____

6. -ate   _____

7. -ation   _____

8. equ/equi   _____

9. -ity   _____

10. -al   _____

D. Writing Sentences

Use each word from the choice box to write a sentence in context so that its meaning is clear to the reader.

exclaim	equation	equivocate	vocalize	proclaim
proclamation	equity	exclamation	equate	vocation

1. _____

_____

_____

2. _____

_____

_____

3. _____

_____

_____

4. _____

_____

_____

5. _____

_____

_____

6. _____

_____

_____

7. _____

_____

_____

8. _____

_____

_____

9. _____

_____

_____

10. _____

_____

_____

E. (optional) Creative Writing

Use some or all of the words from the choice box to write one or more paragraphs or a short story on a separate piece of paper.

Review
Lessons 23 and 24

A. Write each word part from the choice box next to its definition.

viv/vive	con-	dur/dure	voc	equ/equi	-al/i-al	-id
-ly	-able	-ize	pro-	-ity	-acious	en-
-ation	re-	ex-	-ate	vor/vour	claim/clam	

1. _____ out, away, from

2. _____ in, into

3. _____ for, before, forward

4. _____ call out, shout

5. _____ able to be

6. _____ having the quality of

7. _____ back, again

8. _____ harden, to last, lasting

9. _____ live, life

10. _____ like, related to; an action or process

11. _____ an action or process

12. _____ like, related to

13. _____ equal, fair

14. _____ voice, call

15. _____ to make, to act; one who, that which

16. _____ with, together

17. _____ to make, to act

18. _____ state, quality, act

19. _____ in the manner of, having the quality of

B. Write the letter of the correct definition for each word.

WORD		DEFINITION
1. proclaim	_____	(a) fairness; the state of being just or fair
2. durable	_____	(b) a statement of equality
3. vocalize	_____	(c) something announced officially in public
4. exclamation	_____	(d) to cry out or speak in a strong or sudden manner
5. vivid	_____	(e) to use misleading language that could be interpreted in different ways
6. equate	_____	(f) to bring back to life or consciousness
7. revival	_____	(g) to remain, to last
8. duration	_____	(h) in a bright or intense manner
9. vocation	_____	(i) lively, jovial, friendly
10. vivacious	_____	(j) done in a high-spirited manner
11. revive	_____	(k) to make, treat, or regard as equal or equivalent
12. exclaim	_____	(l) an outcry, a shout
13. equity	_____	(m) to announce, to declare, to make public
14. proclamation	_____	(n) to put into words, to utter, to speak
15. convivial	_____	(o) calling, profession, career
16. equivocate	_____	(p) lively in appearance; bright; intense; strong
17. vivaciously	_____	(q) high-spirited and full of life
18. vividly	_____	(r) the length of time something lasts
19. endure	_____	(s) the act of bringing back to life; renewed interest in
20. equation	_____	(t) having the quality of lasting

C. Use the jumbled letters to write the correct word for each definition.

JUMBLED LETTERS	DEFINITION	WORD
1. uiqveceaot	to use misleading language that could be interpreted in different ways	_____
2. avctnooi	calling, profession, career	_____
3. ieervv	to bring back to life or consciousness	_____
4. dbrluae	having the quality of lasting	_____
5. viydivl	in a bright or intense manner	_____
6. xmaceil	to cry out or speak in a strong or sudden manner	_____
7. rtolaomipnac	something announced officially in public	_____
8. nueitaqo	a statement of equality	_____
9. evczailo	to put into words, to utter, to speak	_____
10. deneru	to remain, to last	_____
11. iiacnolvv	lively, jovial, friendly	_____
12. duontrai	the length of time something lasts	_____
13. yqueit	fairness; the state of being just or fair	_____
14. lxtoeaicamn	an outcry, a shout	_____
15. liivuscvyoa	done in a high-spirited manner	_____
16. evvilar	the act of bringing back to life; renewed interest in	_____
17. aimprolc	to announce, to declare, to make public	_____
18. ueqeta	to make, treat, or regard as equal or equivalent	_____
19. ividv	lively in appearance; bright; intense; strong	_____
20. viscaivuo	high-spirited and full of life	_____

D. Write the best word from the gray box to complete each sentence.

1. I don't like to _____ youth with immaturity.

   proclaim   equate   exclaim

2. Picasso's _____ was painting.

   vocation   proclamation   exclamation

3. My raincoat is made of very _____ material.

   vivacious   vivid   durable

4. The repertory company is planning to _____ plays from 30 years ago.

   endure   revive   proclaim

5. Many European structures have had to _____ for centuries.

   endure   equate   revive

6. Suddenly, I heard her _____, "You're a liar!"

   proclaim   exclaim   vocalize

7. The equal sign is important in a mathematical _____.

   proclamation   duration   equation

8. The president will _____ a national day of mourning for the hurricane disaster victims.

   revive   exclaim   proclaim

9. Our new neighbors are very outgoing and _____.

   convivial   durable   vivid

10. It was very enjoyable to see a dance routine done so _____.

   vivid   vividly   vivaciously

D. Write the best word from the gray box to complete each sentence.

11. The factory will remain closed for the _____ of the strike.

    duration   proclamation   revival

12. Don't _____, just give me a straight answer.

    endure   equivocate   vocalize

13. Lacey let out a/an _____ of joy when she heard the good news.

    proclamation   duration   exclamation

14. The soprano tries to _____ for two hours each day.

    vocalize   equivocate   endure

15. The little boy has a _____ imagination.

    vivid   convivial   durable

16. The exciting film caused the _____ of my interest in volcanology.

    duration   proclamation   revival

17. Katelyn saw the _____ in the plan that called for each child to take a turn cleaning the mouse cage.

    equation   equity   duration

18. The sky was filled with _____ shining stars.

    vivaciously   durable   vividly

19. In 1863, President Lincoln issued a/an _____ which freed the slaves.

    proclamation   equation   exclamation

20. The _____ girl made a good cheerleader.

    vivid   durable   vivacious

Lesson 25

PREFIX		ROOT		SUFFIX	
ac-	to, toward, near	cumul	mass, heap	-ary	that which; someone or something that belongs to; of, related to; one who
il-	in, into; not	lumin	light	-ate	to make, to act; one who, that which
				-ation	an action or process
				-escent	becoming, having
				os-ity	state, quality, act
				at-ive	tending to or performing
				-ous	having the quality of
				-us	thing which

A. Spelling and Defining Words

Write each word from the choice box next to its definition.

accumulate	luminary	luminosity	luminescent
cumulative	luminous	illumination	illuminative
illuminate	cumulus		

1. _____   gradually building up

2. _____   to give light to

3. _____   to gather or pile up little by little

4. _____   giving off or reflecting light

5. _____   an object, like a star, that gives off light; a famous person ("star")

6. _____   a heap, a pile, a mass; a thick, puffy type of cloud

7. _____   tending to produce light

8. _____   the relative quantity of light; a state of being luminous

9. _____   glowing, luminous

10. _____   the process of lighting up

B. Completing the Sentence
Write the best word from the gray box to complete each sentence.

1. The _____ stars shone brightly in the dark of night.

   cumulative   illuminate   luminous

2. Julia's scrapbook was a _____ project that took many years to complete.

   luminescent   luminous   cumulative

3. The winner of the game had to _____ the most points.

   illumination   accumulate   illuminate

4. The fans at the famous Hollywood restaurant kept watch for a glimpse of their favorite
   _____.

   cumulus   luminary   illumination

5. They installed spotlights in order to _____ the building.

   illumination   accumulate   illuminate

6. The bright and _____ street light shines through my bedroom window
   at night.

   luminary   cumulative   illuminative

7. Our attic is filled with a _____ of old dolls and toys.

   luminary   cumulus   luminosity

8. My keyboard has a feature that allows me to adjust the _____ of
   my screen.

   luminosity   luminary   cumulus

9. The _____ of the stage was achieved by footlights.

   illumination   luminary   luminosity

10. Children love to watch the _____ light of fireflies.

    cumulative   luminous   luminescent

C. Defining the Word Parts

Write the definition from the choice box next to its correct word part.

- to, toward, near
- out, away, from
- light
- to make, to act; one who, that which
- tending to or performing
- having the quality of
- in, into, not
- mass, heap
- an action or process
- state, quality, act
- thing which
- becoming, having
- that which; someone or something that belongs to; of, related to; one who

1. -us   _____

2. cumul   _____

3. il-   _____

4. -ation   _____

5. os-ity   _____

6. lumin   _____

7. -ary   _____

8. ac-   _____

9. -ate   _____

10. at-ive   _____

11. -ous   _____

12. -escent   _____

D. Writing Sentences

Use each word from the choice box to write a sentence in context so that its meaning is clear to the reader.

accumulate	illuminate	luminous	luminosity	luminescent
cumulative	luminary	cumulus	illumination	illuminative

1. _____

_____

_____

2. _____

_____

_____

3. _____

_____

_____

4. _____

_____

_____

5. _____

_____

_____

6. _____

_____

_____

7. _____

_____

_____

8. _____

_____

_____

9. _____

_____

_____

10. _____

_____

_____

E. (optional) Creative Writing

Use some or all of the words from the choice box to write one or more paragraphs or a short story on a separate piece of paper.

Lesson 26

PREFIX	
in-	in, into; not
ir-	in, into; not
re-	back, again

ROOT	
nov	new
voc/ voci	voice, call

SUFFIX	
-able	able to be
-ate	to make, to act; one who, that which
-ation	an action or process
-ferous	producing
-ice	one who, that which
el-ist	one who
el-ty	state, quality; that which

A. Spelling and Defining Words

Write each word from the choice box next to its definition.

> innovate   renovation   innovation   revocable
> irrevocable   novice   renovate   vociferous
> novelty   novelist

1. _____ to make something like new again

2. _____ loud, noisy

3. _____ the act or process of inventing something new

4. _____ a person who is new to an activity; a beginner

5. _____ able to be repealed or withdrawn

6. _____ one who writes novels

7. _____ to introduce new methods, devices, etc.

8. _____ not subject to reversal

9. _____ the action or process of making something like new again

10. _____ newness, originality

B. Completing the Sentence
Write the best word from the gray box to complete each sentence.

1. The new coach's contract was _____ if he was unable to improve

   the team.

   irrevocable   vociferous   revocable

2. Owners of very old homes often _____ them so they look exactly as they

   did when they were first built.

   revocable   renovate   innovate

3. Making items from plastic was a/an _____ of the 20th century.

   innovation   renovation   novelty

4. The team was _____ when the umpire called their batter out.

   revocable   vociferous   irrevocable

5. Everyone could see Nolan was a _____ when he repeatedly fell off

   the skateboard.

   novelty   novice   novelist

6. The architect will _____ a stylish and unique design for the new

   city hall building.

   renovate   innovate   renovation

7. The _____ of the dilapidated building begins next week.

   renovation   innovation   novelty

8. The court's decision to shut down the unsafe coal mine is _____.

   vociferous   revocable   irrevocable

9. There's little _____ in his writing.

   novelty   renovation   innovation

10. The famous _____ grew up in my own hometown.

    novice   novelty   novelist

C. Defining the Word Parts

Write the definition from the choice box next to its correct word part. A definition may be used more than once.

> - in, into; not
> - back, again
> - new
> - end, limit
> - voice, call
> - able to be
>
> - to make, to act; one who, that which
> - one who
> - state, quality; that which
> - an action or process
> - producing
> - one who, that which

1. el-ist _____

2. re- _____

3. nov _____

4. -able _____

5. ir- _____

6. -ate _____

7. voc/voci _____

8. -ation _____

9. in- _____

10. -ferous _____

11. el-ty _____

12. -ice _____

D. Writing Sentences

Use each word from the choice box to write a sentence in context so that its meaning is clear to the reader.

innovate	novelty	novice	innovation	revocable
irrevocable	renovation	novelist	renovate	vociferous

1. _____

   _____

   _____

2. _____

   _____

   _____

3. _____

   _____

   _____

4. _____

   _____

   _____

5. _____

   _____

   _____

6. _____

   _____

   _____

7. _____

   _____

   _____

8. _____

   _____

   _____

9. _____

   _____

   _____

10. _____

   _____

   _____

E. (optional) Creative Writing

Use some or all of the words from the choice box to write one or more paragraphs or a short story on a separate piece of paper.

Review
Lessons 25 and 26

A. Write each word part from the choice box next to its definition.

cumul	nov	-ary	-ate	-ous	at-ive	-escent	-us
-ation	-able	il-	re-	ir-	ex-	-ice	el-ist
ac-	in-	lumin	voc/voci	-ferous	os-ity	el-ty	

1. _____ to, toward, near

2. _____ light

3. _____ to make, to act; one who, that which

4. _____ tending to or performing

5. _____ having the quality of

6. _____ in, into; not

7. _____ back, again

8. _____ new

9. _____ voice, call

10. _____ able to be

11. _____ in, into; not

12. _____ one who

13. _____ state, quality; that which

14. _____ an action or process

15. _____ producing

16. _____ one who, that which

17. _____ in, into, not

18. _____ mass, heap

19. _____ state, quality, act

20. _____ thing which

21. _____ becoming, having

22. _____ that which; someone or something that belongs to; of, related to; one who

B. Write the letter of the correct definition for each word.

WORD	DEFINITION
1. illuminate _____	(a) a heap, a pile, a mass; a thick, puffy type of cloud
2. novelist _____	(b) tending to produce light
3. innovate _____	(c) the relative quantity of light; a state of being luminous
4. novelty _____	(d) glowing, luminous
5. irrevocable _____	(e) the process of lighting up
6. luminary _____	(f) to make something like new again
7. luminous _____	(g) loud, noisy
8. accumulate _____	(h) the act or process of inventing something new
9. renovation _____	(i) a person who is new to an activity; a beginner
10. cumulative _____	(j) able to be repealed or withdrawn
11. revocable _____	(k) gradually building up
12. cumulus _____	(l) to give light to
13. innovation _____	(m) to gather or pile up little by little
14. vociferous _____	(n) giving off or reflecting light
15. renovate _____	(o) an object, like a star, that gives off light; a famous person ("star")
16. illuminative _____	(p) one who writes novels
17. luminosity _____	(q) to introduce new methods, devices, etc.
18. illumination _____	(r) not subject to reversal
19. novice _____	(s) the action or process of making something like new again
20. luminescent _____	(t) newness, originality

C. Use the jumbled letters to write the correct word for each definition.

JUMBLED LETTERS	DEFINITION	WORD
1. ilnaitvlmieu	tending to produce light	_____
2. ntosevli	one who writes novels	_____
3. ntoninivoa	the act or process of inventing something new	_____
4. elcmaucuta	to gather or pile up little by little	_____
5. tnylove	newness, originality	_____
6. eualvutimc	gradually building up	_____
7. tiilnainuolm	the process of lighting up	_____
8. cniove	a person who is new to an activity; a beginner	_____
9. crievberola	not subject to reversal	_____
10. etevaorn	to make something like new again	_____
11. mitlilnaeu	to give light to	_____
12. menecnliuts	glowing, luminous	_____
13. aboelrevc	able to be repealed or withdrawn	_____
14. ovainetn	to introduce new methods, devices, etc.	_____
15. vorsuoicef	loud, noisy	_____
16. lmaunriy	an object, like a star, that gives off light; a famous person ("star")	_____
17. uuulmsc	a heap, a pile, a mass; a thick, puffy type of cloud	_____
18. unisuoml	giving off or reflecting light	_____
19. ontivneaor	the action or process of making something like new again	_____
20. tonmiyiuls	the relative quantity of light; a state of being luminous	_____

D. Write the best word from the gray box to complete each sentence.

1. Will has more than thirteen years _____ work experience.

   > cumulative   vociferous   luminescent

2. Even though Carmen was a _____, she won the card game.

   > novelist   novelty   novice

3. The store's new scanner was a/an _____ that sped up the checking

   out process.

   > renovation   innovation   novelty

4. Anne's goal was to _____ enough points in the game to win a prize.

   > accumulate   illuminate   renovate

5. A driver's license is _____ if a person gets too many speeding tickets.

   > irrevocable   revocable   cumulative

6. The new owners will _____ the rickety old building.

   > illuminate   innovate   renovate

7. A _____ group of boys rushed into the room.

   > vociferous   luminous   luminescent

8. Torches were used to _____ the picnic grounds.

   > renovate   illuminate   innovate

9. The mashed potatoes on my plate remind me of _____ clouds.

   > illuminative   cumulative   cumulus

10. Some stars have greater _____ than others.

   > luminosity   illumination   innovation

11. Kennedy Middle School plans to _____ a new method of teaching for

advanced students.

renovate   innovate   illuminate

12. The contract was binding and _____.

revocable   cumulative   irrevocable

13. There was much _____ in this season's ballet performances.

novelty   luminosity   illumination

14. The _____ of the old municipal building will be a lengthy project.

innovation   luminosity   renovation

15. The sun is a _____ in the sky.

luminary   cumulus   novelty

16. The many candles at the memorial ceremony were _____ as well

as glowing.

cumulative   vociferous   illuminative

17. My watch has a _____ dial.

revocable   luminous   vociferous

18. The _____ has written many books in which forest animals are the

main characters.

novice   luminary   novelist

19. The library's computer rooms need better _____.

illumination   renovation   innovation

20. At night our cat's eyes are _____.

vociferous   luminescent   cumulative

Lesson 27

PREFIX	
con-	with, together
ex-	out, away, from
se-	apart, aside

ROOT	
clude/ clus	close
herbi	grass
vor	eat

SUFFIX	
-cide	kill
-ion	an action or process; state, quality, act
-ive	tending to or perfroming
-ous	having the quality of

A. Spelling and Defining Words

Write each word from the choice box next to its definition.

conclusion   herbicide   exclusive   exclude
exclusion   herbivorous   conclusive   seclusion
seclude   conclude

1. _____   plant-eating

2. _____   the end or last part

3. _____   to keep away from; to isolate

4. _____   a shutting out; rejection

5. _____   any chemical used to kill unwanted plants, etc.

6. _____   to bring to a close; end; finish

7. _____   shutting or ruling out other options, tending to shut out others

8. _____   that which settles a question; decisive; final

9. _____   to shut or rule out; to refuse to admit or include

10. _____   isolation; a shutting off or keeping away from others

B. Completing the Sentence

Write the best word from the gray box to complete each sentence.

1. The _____ of short children from the team seemed unfair to Thomas.

    conclusion   seclusion   exclusion

2. The actress felt compelled to _____ herself from her fans.

    conclude   exclude   seclude

3. They had to be careful when applying the _____ to the lawn.

    herbicide   seclusion   conclusion

4. The play had an unexpected _____.

    exclusion   conclusion   seclusion

5. Some animals in the wild are _____, while others are flesh-eating.

    herbivorous   exclusive   conclusive

6. We enjoy our mountain cabin because of its _____.

    conclusion   exclusion   seclusion

7. The pianist will _____ the recital with a piece from Chopin.

    seclude   conclude   exclude

8. The company had the _____ right to sell their products.

    exclusive   conclusive   herbivorous

9. The men's bowling league decided to _____ males under the age of 18.

    seclude   conclude   exclude

10. Fingerprints on the gun were _____ evidence that the suspect was guilty.

    conclusive   exclusive   herbivorous

C. Defining the Word Parts

Write the definition from the choice box next to its correct word part.

> • with, together
> • out, away, from
> • apart, aside
> • spirit, life
> • tending to or performing
> • close
>
> • kill
> • grass
> • an action or process; state, quality, act
> • having the quality of
> • eat

1. -cide _____

2. con- _____

3. herbi _____

4. se- _____

5. -ion _____

6. clude/clus _____

7. ex- _____

8. vor _____

9. -ive _____

10. -ous _____

D. Writing Sentences

Use each word from the choice box to write a sentence in context so that its meaning is clear to the reader.

conclusion	seclude	herbivorous	exclusive	exclude
exclusion	herbicide	conclude	conclusive	seclusion

1. _____

_____

_____

2. _____

_____

_____

3. _____

_____

_____

4. _____

_____

_____

5. _____

_____

_____

6. _____

_____

_____

7. _____

_____

_____

8. _____

_____

_____

9. _____

_____

_____

10. _____

_____

_____

E. (optional) Creative Writing

Use some or all of the words from the choice box to write one or more paragraphs or a short story on a separate piece of paper.

Lesson 28

PREFIX	
con-	with, together
dis-	apart, opposite of
ultra-	beyond
uni-	one

ROOT	
form	shape, form
son	sound
tort	twist

SUFFIX	
-ance	state, quality, act
-ant	one who, that which; state, quality
-ation	an action or process
-ic	like, related to
-ion	an action or process; state, quality, act

A. Spelling and Defining Words

Write each word from the choice box next to its definition.

> dissonance   contortion   contort   distortion
> ultrasonic   distort   uniform   formation
> unison   dissonant

1. _____ a twisted shape or position

2. _____ as one voice

3. _____ lack of harmony; discord

4. _____ to alter the shape or condition of

5. _____ related to a frequency of sound vibrations beyond the normal hearing range; high in frequency

6. _____ to twist from its usual shape or position

7. _____ characterized by a lack of harmony; discordant

8. _____ the process of shaping, forming, or establishing

9. _____ the process of altering the shape or condition of

10. _____ equal, at one, consistent

B. Completing the Sentence
Write the best word from the gray box to complete each sentence.

1. The _____ behavior of some family members made the reunion
   very unpleasant.
   > ultrasonic   distortion   dissonant

2. The windows in our house are all _____.
   > uniform   contort   distort

3. Excruciating pain caused him to _____ his facial expressions.
   > contort   distort   uniform

4. The _____ of the pictures was due to a defective camera lens.
   > dissonance   formation   distortion

5. The pilgrims' goal was the _____ of a colony in the New World.
   > formation   unison   distortion

6. The acrobat's _____ was amazing to watch.
   > dissonance   contortion   unison

7. Animal trainers use _____ whistles to train dogs and dolphins.
   > dissonant   contortion   ultrasonic

8. No one wanted to be Jack's friend because he would _____ the truth to
   get his way.
   > contort   uniform   distort

9. The chorus sang the song in _____.
   > contortion   unison   dissonance

10. The _____ between the strings and horns made it difficult to listen
    to the performance.
    > dissonance   formation   distortion

C. Defining the Word Parts

Write the definition from the choice box next to its correct word part.

- an action or process
- shape, form
- one who, that which; state, quality
- remember
- with, together
- apart, opposite of
- sound
- one
- beyond
- twist
- state, quality, act
- like, related to
- an action or process; state, quality, act

1. dis- _____

2. -ant _____

3. son _____

4. -ation _____

5. -ic _____

6. con- _____

7. -ance _____

8. ultra- _____

9. tort _____

10. form _____

11. uni- _____

12. -ion _____

D. Writing Sentences

Use each word from the choice box to write a sentence in context so that its meaning is clear to the reader.

dissonance	unison	distort	contort	distortion
ultrasonic	contortion	dissonant	uniform	formation

1. _____

   _____

   _____

2. _____

   _____

   _____

3. _____

   _____

   _____

4. _____

   _____

   _____

5. _____

   _____

   _____

6. _____

   _____

   _____

7. _____

   _____

   _____

8. _____

   _____

   _____

9. _____

   _____

   _____

10. _____

    _____

    _____

E. (optional) Creative Writing

Use some or all of the words from the choice box to write one or more paragraphs or a short story on a separate piece of paper.

Review
Lessons 27 and 28

A. Write each word part from the choice box next to its definition.

-ion	clude/clus	re-	-ance	herbi	-ous	-ation
con-	son	tort	-ic	vor	-ive	-ant
dis-	ex-	ultra-	se-	-cide	uni-	form

1. _____ beyond

2. _____ one

3. _____ sound

4. _____ twist

5. _____ state, quality, act

6. _____ tending to or performing

7. _____ an action or process; state, quality, act

8. _____ with, together

9. _____ apart, opposite of

10. _____ like, related to

11. _____ out, away, from

12. _____ apart, aside

13. _____ close

14. _____ grass

15. _____ eat

16. _____ kill

17. _____ an action or process

18. _____ having the quality of

19. _____ shape, form

20. _____ one who, that which; state, quality

B. Write the letter of the correct definition for each word.

WORD		DEFINITION
1. conclusive _____	(a)	a twisted shape or position
2. exclude _____	(b)	as one voice
3. conclude _____	(c)	lack of harmony; discord
4. seclusion _____	(d)	to alter the shape or condition of
5. formation _____	(e)	related to a frequency of sound vibrations beyond the normal hearing range; high in frequency
6. exclusive _____	(f)	plant-eating
7. contort _____	(g)	the end or last part
8. uniform _____	(h)	to keep away from; to isolate
9. dissonant _____	(i)	a shutting out; rejection
10. distortion _____	(j)	any chemical used to kill unwanted plants, etc.
11. conclusion _____	(k)	to twist from its usual shape or position
12. exclusion _____	(l)	characterized by a lack of harmony; discordant
13. seclude _____	(m)	equal, at one, consistent
14. herbicide _____	(n)	the process of altering the shape or condition of
15. ultrasonic _____	(o)	the process of shaping, forming, or establishing
16. dissonance _____	(p)	to bring to a close; end; finish
17. herbivorous _____	(q)	shutting or ruling out other options, tending to shut out others
18. contortion _____	(r)	which settles a question; decisive; final
19. unison _____	(s)	to shut or rule out; to refuse to admit or include
20. distort _____	(t)	isolation; a shutting off or keeping away from others

C. Use the jumbled letters to write the correct word for each definition.

JUMBLED LETTERS	DEFINITION	WORD
1. ssuicolen	isolation; a shutting off or keeping away from others	_____
2. nofaitrom	the process of shaping, forming, or establishing	_____
3. eedxlcu	to shut or rule out; to refuse to admit or include	_____
4. stidort	to alter the shape or condition of	_____
5. oneisuvclc	that which settles a question; decisive; final	_____
6. otinntcroo	a twisted shape or position	_____
7. vicuelexs	shutting or ruling out other options, tending to shut out others	_____
8. usnnoi	as one voice	_____
9. elcudcno	to bring to a close; end; finish	_____
10. cauonlirts	related to a frequency of sound vibrations beyond the normal hearing range; high in frequency	_____
11. rrhisoveuob	plant-eating	_____
12. nessaconid	lack of harmony; discord	_____
13. dsceuel	to keep away from; to isolate	_____
14. tionoitdsr	the process of altering the shape or condition of	_____
15. cxlonesui	a shutting out; rejection	_____
16. dsitnnosa	characterized by a lack of harmony; discordant	_____
17. ebeihdirc	any chemical used to kill unwanted plants, etc.	_____
18. niurofm	equal, at one, consistent	_____
19. ctnootr	to twist from its usual shape or position	_____
20. siolcoucnn	the end or last part	_____

D. Write the best word from the gray box to complete each sentence.

1. Bats give off _____ calls to help them locate their food.

   dissonant ultrasonic conclusive

2. Evan's bodily _____ made him look like a human pretzel.

   contortion exclusion uniform

3. The brothers were united at the _____ of the book.

   seclusion exclusion conclusion

4. _____ animals typically have mouthparts adapted to rasping or grinding.

   Herbivorous Ultrasonic Dissonant

5. The dignitaries managed to _____ the peace negotiations successfully.

   exclude distort conclude

6. The little girl had the amazing ability to _____ her body.

   contort exclude distort

7. The North Bend school board agreed to the _____ of the student
   representative committee.

   dissonance unison formation

8. The realtor had the right to sell the building to the _____ of all others.

   exclusion dissonance conclusion

9. The _____ sound of the chorus was harsh to the ears.

   ultrasonic exclusive dissonant

10. The bias of a reporter can easily _____ the news.

    contort distort seclude

D. (continued) Write the best word from the gray box to complete each sentence.

11. The best way to keep the two biggest guinea pigs calm is to _____ them

from the others.

seclude   distort   conclude

12. I'd much rather pull the weeds than use a harmful _____.

formation   herbicide   conclusion

13. The club was so _____ only the very rich could join.

conclusive   dissonant   exclusive

14. Arthritis caused the _____ of Wyatt's fingers.

distortion   unison   seclusion

15. Their shout of goodbye was done in _____.

unison   seclusion   dissonance

16. The students gave a/an _____ argument for needing a class president.

dissonant   exclusive   conclusive

17. The acoustics are _____ throughout the auditorium.

ultrasonic   dissonant   uniform

18. The band needed a lot of practice due to the _____ in the sound quality.

dissonance   unison   distortion

19.   The eccentric millionaire went into _____ to avoid the media.

seclusion   formation   exclusion

20. The doctor was able to _____ food poisoning as the cause of Elena's

sudden illness.

seclude   exclude   contort

Lesson 29

PREFIX	
en-	in, into
in-	in, into; not
retro-	backward

ROOT	
spec/ spect	look, examine
vis	see

SUFFIX	
ific-ation	an action or process
i-fy	to make, to act, to do
-ible	able to be
-ion	an action or process; state, quality, act
-ive	tending to or performing

A. Spelling and Defining Words

Write each word from the choice box next to its definition.

> inspection   envision   visible   retrospection
> retrospect   invisible   specification   retrospective
> specify   inspect

1. _____ to picture in the mind

2. _____ impossible to see

3. _____ to state in detail or name

4. _____ the remembering of past events

5. _____ the act of examining or reviewing

6. _____ to examine, to look over carefully

7. _____ able to be seen

8. _____ looking back on the past or past events

9. _____ the process of stating in detail; requirement; stipulation

10. _____ the act of looking back on past events, experiences, etc.

B. Completing the Sentence
Write the best word from the gray box to complete each sentence.

1. The colorful brochures helped them _____ what Walt Disney World® would be like.

   specify inspect envision

2. Marina worked an hour cleaning her room and hoped that it would pass her mother's _____.

   specification retrospection inspection

3. They asked Josiah to _____ the exact time and place of his arrival at the train station.

   specify envision inspect

4. It was so foggy that the house next door was _____.

   visible invisible retrospective

5. In _____, the injured skier wished he had remained on the beginner's slope.

   specification inspection retrospect

6. How often does the auditor _____ the books?

   inspect specify envision

7. The vague charges against the suspect lacked _____.

   retrospection specification inspection

8. The _____ exhibit honored the lifetime achievements of the deceased artist.

   visible invisible retrospective

9. Even though the wind blew and there were no _____ defects, the kite still wouldn't fly.

   invisible visible retrospective

10. Each episode of the miniseries begins with a/an _____ of the previous one.

   specification inspection retrospection

C. Defining the Word Parts
Write the definition from the choice box next to its correct word part.

> - state, quality, act
> - in, into
> - look, examine
> - able to be
> - in, into; not
> - backward
> - see
> - to make, to act, to do
> - an action or process; state, quality, act
> - tending to or performing
> - an action or process

1. i-fy _____

2. en- _____

3. vis _____

4. ific-ation _____

5. in- _____

6. -ible _____

7. spec/spect _____

8. retro- _____

9. -ion _____

10. -ive _____

D. Writing Sentences

Use each word from the choice box to write a sentence in context so that its meaning is clear to the reader.

inspection	specify	invisible	visible	retrospection
retrospect	envision	inspect	specification	retrospective

1. _____

   _____

   _____

2. _____

   _____

   _____

3. _____

   _____

   _____

4. _____

   _____

   _____

5. _____

   _____

   _____

6. _____

   _____

   _____

7. _____

   _____

   _____

8. _____

   _____

   _____

9. _____

   _____

   _____

10. _____

    _____

    _____

E. (optional) Creative Writing

Use some or all of the words from the choice box to write one or more paragraphs or a short story on a separate piece of paper.

Lesson 30

PREFIX	
ad-	to, toward, near
dis-	apart, opposite of
e-	out, away, from
inter-	between, among
re-	back, again

ROOT	
miss/ mit/ mitt	send, let go
sect	cut

SUFFIX	
-ance	state, quality, act
-ary	that which; someone or something that belongs to; of, related to; one who
-ion	an action or process; state, quality, act

A. Spelling and Defining Words

Write each word from the choice box next to its definition.

admit	dissect	intermission	intersect
emissary	intersection	remit	dissection
remittance	admission		

1. _____ let enter, give access to

2. _____ to cut apart piece by piece

3. _____ interval of time between period of activity; a pause

4. _____ the act of sending back money to pay

5. _____ entry; entrance fee

6. _____ the place or point where two things cross each other

7. _____ a representative of a country or group sent on a mission

8. _____ discharge; pardon; set free, release

9. _____ to cut across, traverse

10. _____ an analysis part by part, a detailed examination

B. Completing the Sentence
Write the best word from the gray box to complete each sentence.

1. The two roads _____ a mile from here.

    dissect   remit   intersect

2. The children were told to cross the street only at the _____.

    intersection   intermission   dissection

3. It shouldn't be too difficult to _____ an accidental unkindness.

    remit   intersect   dissect

4. Each country sent a/an _____ to the world peace meeting.

    emissary   remittance   dissection

5. Please _____ the guests of honor.

    intersect   dissect   admit

6. The _____ of the poem helped me understand the author's meaning.

    intersection   dissection   intermission

7. The play's first _____ will last ten minutes.

    admission   intermission   intersection

8. The botany class had already begun to _____ the flowers.

    intersect   admit   dissect

9. We prefer to pay our bills by electronic _____.

    admission   remittance   intersection

10. _____ to the show is $15.00.

    Admission   Intermission   Remittance

C. Defining the Word Parts
Write the definition from the choice box next to its correct word part.

- to, toward, near
- cut
- state, quality, act
- place, put
- apart, opposite of
- out, away, from

- between, among
- back, again
- send, let go
- that which; someone or something that belongs to; of, related to, one who
- an action or process; state, quality, act

1. -ary _____

2. e- _____

3. inter- _____

4. sect _____

5. ad- _____

6. miss/mit/mitt _____

7. -ance _____

8. -ion _____

9. re- _____

10. dis- _____

D. Writing Sentences

Use each word from the choice box to write a sentence in context so that its meaning is clear to the reader.

admit	remittance	intersection	intermission	intersect
emissary	dissect	admission	remit	dissection

1. _____

_____

_____

2. _____

_____

_____

3. _____

_____

_____

4. _____

_____

_____

5. _____

_____

_____

6. _____

_____

_____

7. _____

_____

_____

8. _____

_____

_____

9. _____

_____

_____

10. _____

_____

_____

E. (optional) Creative Writing

Use some or all of the words from the choice box to write one or more paragraphs or a short story on a separate piece of paper.

Review
Lessons 29 and 30

A. Write each word part from the choice box next to its definition.

i-fy	ific-ation	dis-	-ion	e-	ad-	-ous
en-	in-	spec/spect	-ive	inter-	-ance	re-
vis	-ible	retro-	-ary	sect	miss/mit/mitt	

1. _____ to, toward, near

2. _____ cut

3. _____ state, quality, act

4. _____ in, into

5. _____ look, examine

6. _____ able to be

7. _____ in, into; not

8. _____ backward

9. _____ see

10. _____ to make, to act, to do

11. _____ an action or process; state, quality, act

12. _____ tending to or performing

13. _____ apart, opposite of

14. _____ out, away, from

15. _____ between, among

16. _____ back, again

17. _____ that which; someone or something that belongs to; of, related to, one who

18. _____ an action or process

19. _____ send, let go

B. Write the letter of the correct definition for each word.

WORD		DEFINITION
1. envision	_____	(a) entry; entrance fee
2. specify	_____	(b) interval of time between period of activity; a pause
3. dissect	_____	(c) discharge; pardon; set free, release
4. invisible	_____	(d) to cut across, traverse
5. emissary	_____	(e) an analysis part by part, a detailed examination
6. retrospect	_____	(f) to examine, to look over carefully
7. inspection	_____	(g) able to be seen
8. admit	_____	(h) looking back on the past or past events
9. remittance	_____	(i) the process of stating in detail; requirement; stipulation
10. intersection	_____	(j) the act of looking back on past events, experiences, etc.
11. specification	_____	(k) the act of sending back money to pay
12. remit	_____	(l) to cut apart piece by piece
13. retrospective	_____	(m) let enter, give access to
14. retrospection	_____	(n) the place or point where two things cross each other
15. dissection	_____	(o) a representative of a country or group sent on a mission
16. admission	_____	(p) to picture in the mind
17. intersect	_____	(q) impossible to see
18. intermission	_____	(r) to state in detail or name
19. inspect	_____	(s) the remembering of past events
20. visible	_____	(t) the act of examining or reviewing

C. Use the jumbled letters to write the correct word for each definition.

JUMBLED LETTERS	DEFINITION	WORD
1. sdenciiots	an analysis part by part, a detailed examination	_____
2. dmiat	let enter, give access to	_____
3. peoicstnin	the act of examining or reviewing	_____
4. reicosrvpteet	looking back on the past or past events	_____
5. ctnsetrie	to cut across, traverse	_____
6. yasmrsei	a representative of a country or group sent on a mission	_____
7. rptcrsetoe	the remembering of past events	_____
8. iifonsaietpcc	the process of stating in detail; requirement; stipulation	_____
9. ecterintma	the act of sending back money to pay	_____
10. isanoidms	entry; entrance fee	_____
11. coonsprieetrt	the act of looking back on past events, experiences, etc.	_____
12. syefpic	to state in detail or name	_____
13. enisvnoi	to picture in the mind	_____
14. snvieilbi	impossible to see	_____
15. rietm	discharge; pardon; set free, release	_____
16. icdests	to cut apart piece by piece	_____
17. triosinneetc	the place or point where two things cross each other	_____
18. isilbev	able to be seen	_____
19. imssnroiietn	interval of time between period of activity; a pause	_____
20. tsneipc	to examine, to look over carefully	_____

D. Write the best word from the gray box to complete each sentence.

1. Bert's youth was more enjoyable in _____ than when he was actually going through it.

   remittance retrospect specification

2. The judge will _____ the prisoner if found to be innocent.

   remit admit inspect

3. Please _____ what the job will entail.

   envision remit specify

4. _____ is limited to persons whose names are on the guest list.

   Admission Inspection Intermission

5. The lines _____ at right angles.

   intersect dissect inspect

6. The prime minister met with the queen's _____.

   remittance retrospection emissary

7. The park is _____ from our house.

   retrospective visible retrospect

8. The emergency crew worked all night without _____.

   intermission admission specification

9. Molly fits all but one _____ for the job.

   admission retrospection specification

10. Try to _____ yourself on a sunny beach in the Bahamas.

    envision specify remit

11. H.G. Wells wrote a famous story about a/an _____ man.

retrospective invisible visible

12. We would like your _____ upon receipt of the bill.

remittance inspection intersection

13. The new legislature did a thorough _____ of the bylaws.

dissection remittance inspection

14. The ticket will _____ just one person.

remit admit specify

15. We will _____ a frog in biology class tomorrow.

dissect intersect remit

16. Be sure to have the mechanic _____ the tires too.

remit intersect inspect

17. The truck driver located the _____ of Highway 28 and Highway 60 on his GPS.

intersection intermission dissection

18. Once the organ specimen is received, the lab will begin the process of _____.

retrospection intersection dissection

19. Olivia is a person who lives in anticipation of the future and not in _____.

retrospection admission inspection

20. My uncle considers himself to be a/an _____ octogenarian.

visible retrospective invisible

Answer Key

...act
2. infrastructure
3. construction
4. destruction
5. reconstruct
6. structure
7. obstruction
8. reconstruction
9. obstruct
10. construct

B. (p. 2)
1. destruction
2. obstruction
3. reconstruction
4. infrastructure
5. construct
6. construction
7. structure
8. obstruct
9. destruct
10. reconstruct

C. (p. 3)
1. an action or process; state, quality, act
2. build
3. back, again
4. from, away, down, apart; not
5. beneath
6. state, quality, act; that which; process, condition
7. with, together
8. to, toward, against

D. (p. 4)
Sentences will vary.

E. (p. 4)
Paragraphs will vary.

Lesson 2
A. (p. 5)
1. extract
2. contract
3. extractible
4. extraction
5. invincible
6. convince
7. convincible
8. retract
9. retraction
10. contraction

B. (p. 6)
1. contraction
2. convince
3. extraction
4. invincible
5. retract
6. contract
7. extract
8. extractible
9. convincible
10. retraction

C. (p. 7)
1. in, into; not
2. to draw of pull, drag, draw out
3. an action or process; state, quality, act
4. with, together
5. able to be
6. conquer
7. out, away, from
8. back, again

D. (p. 8)
Sentences will vary.

E. (p. 8)
Paragraphs will vary.

Review Lessons 1 and 2
A. (p. 9)
1. re-
2. ob-
3. de-
4. con-
5. ex-
6. infra-
7. in-
8. -ible
9. vinc/vince
10. -ion
11. struct
12. tract
13. -ure

B. (p. 10)
1. i
2. p
3. n
4. k
5. a
6. t
7. b
8. q
9. c
10. s
11. r
12. d
13. e
14. h
15. f
16. j
17. l
18. g
19. o
20. m

C. (p. 11)
1. reconstruction
2. contraction
3. invincible
4. obstruct

5. retraction
6. extraction
7. construct
8. structure
9. convince
10. retract
11. extractible
12. construction
13. infrastructure
14. reconstruct
15. convincible
16. destruction
17. contract
18. obstruction
19. extract
20. destruct

D. (p.12)
1. obstruction
2. destruction
3. invincible
4. structure
5. extract
6. infrastructure
7. retract
8. construction
9. convincible
10. reconstruct
11. construct
12. retraction
13. extractible
14. contraction
15. convince
16. extraction
17. reconstruction
18. contract
19. obstruct
20. destruct

Lesson 3
A. (p. 14)
1. removable
2. commotion
3. immobile
4. promotion
5. mobility
6. immovable
7. movable
8. immobility
9. promote
10. mobile

B. (p. 15)
1. immobile
2. mobility
3. promotion
4. immovable

5. commotion
6. removable
7. promote
8. immobility
9. movable
10. mobile

C. (p. 16)
1. back, again
2. able to be
3. with, together
4. in, into; not
5. like, of, relating to
6. for, before, forward
7. an action or process; state, quality, act
8. move
9. state, quality, act

D. (p. 17)
Sentences will vary.

E. (p. 17)
Paragraphs will vary.

Lesson 4
A. (p. 18)
1. abbreviate
2. process
3. secession
4. brevity
5. accessible
6. proceed
7. secede
8. procession
9. processable
10. accede

B. (p. 19)
1. secede
2. proceed
3. processable
4. abbreviate
5. accessible
6. accede
7. process
8. secession
9. brevity
10. procession

C. (p. 20)
1. able to be
2. away, from
3. short
4. to, toward, near
5. an action or process; state, quality, act
6. for, before, forward
7. able to be
8. go, yield

   9. apart, aside
  10. to make, to act; one who, that which
  11. state, quality, act

D. (p. 21)
    Sentences will vary.

E. (p. 21)
    Paragraphs will vary.

Review Lessons 3 and 4

A. (p. 22)

1. re-	9. -ion
2. ac-	10. -ile
3. i-ate	11. pro-
4. com-	12. se-
5. ab-	13. -ible or -able
6. im-	14. brev
7. -able or -ible	15. cede/ceed/ cess
8. mob/mot/ mote/mov	16. -ity/il-ity

B. (p. 23)

1. h	11. i
2. m	12. q
3. t	13. j
4. a	14. d
5. f	15. n
6. e	16. r
7. l	17. c
8. p	18. b
9. k	19. g
10. s	20. o

C. (p. 24)
   1. procession
   2. promote
   3. mobile
   4. commotion
   5. immobile
   6. processable
   7. immovable
   8. promotion
   9. secession
  10. removable
  11. mobility
  12. process
  13. secede
  14. abbreviate
  15. proceed
  16. brevity
  17. accessible
  18. accede
  19. immobility
  20. movable

D. (p. 25)
   1. promotion
   2. immobile
   3. brevity
   4. mobile
   5. promote
   6. commotion
   7. mobility
   8. abbreviate
   9. accessible
  10. proceed
  11. immobility
  12. movable
  13. removable
  14. secede
  15. processable
  16. procession
  17. immovable
  18. secession
  19. process
  20. accede

Lesson 5

A. (p. 27)
   1. decelerate
   2. digression
   3. progress
   4. regression
   5. accelerate
   6. digress
   7. deceleration
   8. regress
   9. progression
  10. acceleration

B. (p. 28)
   1. decelerate
   2. digression
   3. accelerate
   4. progress
   5. regression
   6. digress
   7. progression
   8. acceleration
   9. regress
  10. deceleration

C. (p. 29)
   1. an action or process; state, quality, act
   2. to, toward, near
   3. fast
   4. to make, to act; one who, that which
   5. step
   6. back, again
   7. for, before, forward
   8. from, away, down, apart; not
   9. an action or process

10. apart, away; not

D. (p. 30)
    Sentences will vary.

E. (p. 30)
    Paragraphs will vary.

Lesson 6
A. (p. 31)
    1. memorial
    2. aviary
    3. aviatrix
    4. commemorate
    5. memory
    6. aviator
    7. aviation
    8. memorize
    9. memorable
    10. memorization

B. (p. 32)
    1. aviary
    2. commemorate
    3. aviatrix
    4. memory
    5. memorial
    6. aviation
    7. memorable
    8. memorize
    9. aviator
    10. Memorization

C. (p. 33)
    1. like, related to; an action or process
    2. remember
    3. bird
    4. with, together
    5. able to be
    6. that which; someone or something that belongs to; related to; one who
    7. one who, that which; condition, state, activity
    8. feminine
    9. an action or process
    10. to make, to act; one who, that which
    11. to make, to act
    12. state of, quality, act; body, group

D. (p. 34)
    Sentences will vary.

E. (p. 34)
    Paragraphs will vary.

Review Lessons 5 and 6
A. (p. 35)
    1. -ate
    2. celer
    3. ac-
    4. iz-ation or -ation
    5. di-
    6. re-
    7. pro-
    8. de-
    9. -ion
    10. gress
    11. -able
    12. -ation or iz-ation
    13. com-
    14. avi/avia
    15. at-or
    16. i-al
    17. memor
    18. -trix
    19. -y
    20. -ary
    21. -ize

B. (p. 36)
    1. g
    2. o
    3. h
    4. k
    5. f
    6. c
    7. q
    8. t
    9. d
    10. b
    11. s
    12. e
    13. r
    14. a
    15. l
    16. i
    17. j
    18. m
    19. p
    20. n

C. (p. 37)
    1. progression
    2. memorable
    3. accelerate
    4. aviary
    5. digress
    6. memorization
    7. decelerate
    8. aviatrix
    9. regress
    10. acceleration
    11. commemorate
    12. digression
    13. deceleration
    14. aviator
    15. memorize
    16. progress
    17. memory
    18. aviation
    19. regression
    20. memorial

D. (p. 38)
    1. aviary
    2. memorial
    3. decelerate
    4. regression
    5. aviatrix
    6. accelerate
    7. memory
    8. progress

9. commemorate
10. digression
11. acceleration
12. memorable
13. digress
14. aviator
15. memorization
16. regress
17. aviation
18. memorize
19. progression
20. deceleration

Lesson 7
A. (p. 40)
1. aquarium
2. repugnant
3. marine
4. pugilist
5. submarine
6. aquatic
7. aquamarine
8. pugnacious
9. pugilism
10. aqueous

B. (p. 41)
1. marine
2. pugnacious
3. submarine
4. repugnant
5. aquamarine
6. aquatic
7. pugilist
8. aquarium
9. pugilism
10. aqueous

C. (p. 42)
1. like, related to
2. back, again
3. place where
4. like, having the quality of
5. fight
6. under, below
7. having the quality of
8. one who, that which; state, quality
9. water
10. act, state, condition
11. like, related to
12. sea
13. one who

D. (p. 43)
Sentences will vary.

E. (p. 43)
Paragraphs will vary.

Lesson 8
A. (p. 44)
1. inaudible
2. counteract
3. reaction
4. interaction
5. audience
6. audible
7. react
8. counteraction
9. interact
10. inaction

B. (p. 45)
1. reaction
2. interaction
3. audience
4. counteract
5. inaudible
6. inaction
7. audible
8. react
9. interact
10. counteraction

C. (p. 46)
1. an action or process; state, quality, act
2. in, into; not
3. hear
4. against, opposite
5. to do, to drive
6. able to be
7. state, quality, act
8. between, among
9. back, again

D. (p. 47)
Sentences will vary.

E. (p. 47)
Paragraphs will vary.

Review Lessons 7 and 8
A. (p. 48)
1. -acious
2. t-ic or -ine
3. aqu/aqua
4. re-
5. inter-
6. il-ism
7. il-ist
8. mar
9. sub-
10. -arium
11. -ant
12. -ine or t-ic
13. -eous
14. pug/pugn
15. i-ence
16. counter
17. act
18. -ible
19. in-
20. aud
21. -ion

B. (p. 49)

1. i
2. j
3. m
4. p
5. q
6. o
7. t
8. n
9. a
10. b
11. s
12. r
13. c
14. h
15. f
16. d
17. e
18. l
19. k
20. g

C. (p. 50)

1. aqueous
2. repugnant
3. counteraction
4. audible
5. marine
6. aquatic
7. pugilism
8. interaction
9. audience
10. aquamarine
11. pugilist
12. aquarium
13. counteract
14. inaudible
15. react
16. submarine
17. inaction
18. interact
19. pugnacious
20. reaction

D. (p. 51)

1. repugnant
2. interaction
3. inaction
4. aquatic
5. audible
6. pugnacious
7. audience
8. marine
9. aquarium
10. reaction
11. react
12. submarine
13. inaudible
14. interact
15. pugilist
16. aquamarine
17. counteract
18. pugilism
19. aqueous
20. counteraction

Lesson 9

A. (p. 53)

1. juvenile
2. rejuvenate
3. circumvent
4. convention
5. intervene
6. circumvention
7. convent
8. convene
9. intervention
10. circumventive

B. (p. 54)

1. circumvent
2. intervene
3. rejuvenate
4. juvenile
5. convention
6. convene
7. intervention
8. convent
9. circumventive
10. circumvention

C. (p. 55)

1. back, again
2. young
3. to make, to act; one who, that which
4. around
5. come
6. like, of, relating to
7. with, together
8. between, among
9. an action or process; state, quality, act
10. tending to or performing

D. (p. 56)
Sentences will vary.

E. (p. 56)
Paragraphs will vary.

Lesson 10

A. (p. 57)

1. recognize
2. cognition
3. exterminate
4. determination
5. terminal
6. cognitive
7. recognition
8. cognizant
9. extermination
10. terminate

B. (p. 58)
1. terminal
2. determination
3. recognize
4. exterminate
5. cognition
6. terminate
7. extermination
8. recognition
9. cognizant
10. cognitive

C. (p. 59)
1. one who, that which; state, quality
2. to make, to act; one who, that which
3. know
4. like, related to; an action or process
5. back, again
6. tending to or performing
7. end, limit
8. to make, to act; one who, that which
9. out, away, from
10. to make, to act
11. state, quality, act
12. an action or process

D. (p. 60)
Sentences will vary.

E. (p. 60)
Paragraphs will vary.

Review Lessons 9 and 10
A. (p. 61)
1. -ation
2. termin
3. -ize
4. i-tion
5. iz-ant
6. -ive/it-ive
7. juven
8. inter-
9. -ile
10. vene/vent
11. re-
12. -ion
13. ex-
14. -al
15. de-
16. cogn
17. -ate
18. con-
19. circum-

B. (p. 62)
1. h
2. k
3. m
4. o
5. r
6. p
7. q
8. a
9. t
10. s
11. b
12. n
13. c
14. l
15. d
16. f
17. g
18. e
19. j
20. i

C. (p. 63)
1. cognition
2. terminate
3. juvenile
4. circumvention
5. recognize
6. extermination
7. cognitive
8. rejuvenate
9. circumvent
10. convene
11. determination
12. recognition
13. terminal
14. intervene
15. convent
16. cognizant
17. exterminate
18. convention
19. circumventive
20. intervention

D. (p. 64)
1. determination
2. rejuvenate
3. exterminate
4. convene
5. circumventive
6. extermination
7. cognizant
8. convent
9. cognitive
10. recognize
11. recognition
12. juvenile
13. circumvent
14. intervene
15. terminate
16. circumvention
17. convention
18. terminal
19. intervention
20. cognition

Lesson 11
A. (p. 66)
1. describe
2. prescription
3. inscription
4. circumscribe
5. postscript
6. circumscriptive
7. prescribe
8. description
9. inscribe
10. descriptive

B. (p. 67)
1. postscript
2. circumscribe
3. inscription
4. prescription
5. describe
6. circumscriptive
7. description
8. prescribe
9. Inscribe
10. descriptive

C. (p. 68)
1. from, away, down, apart; not
2. tending to or performing
3. write, written
4. around
5. in, into; not
6. before, in front of
7. an action or process; state, quality, act
8. after

D. (p. 69)
Sentences will vary.

E. (p. 69)
Paragraphs will vary.

Lesson 12
A. (p. 70)
1. contact
2. tactile
3. intercept
4. recapture
5. intact
6. capture
7. receptive
8. receptor
9. interceptor
10. interceptive

B. (p. 71)
1. intact
2. recapture
3. intercept
4. contact
5. tactile
6. capture
7. receptive
8. interceptor
9. receptor
10. Interceptive

C. (p. 72)
1. like, of, relating to
2. with, together
3. touch

4. state, quality, act, that which; process, condition
5. in, into; not
6. tending to or performing
7. back, again
8. between, among
9. take, hold
10. one who, that which; condition, state, activity

D. (p. 73)
Sentences will vary.

E. (p. 73)
Paragraphs will vary.

Review Lessons 11 and 12
A. (p. 74)
1. circum-
2. scribe/script
3. -ion
4. de-
5. con-
6. capt/cept
7. -ile
8. in-
9. inter-
10. tact
11. -ure
12. re-
13. post-
14. pre-
15. -ive
16. -or

B. (p. 75)
1. i
2. p
3. t
4. o
5. l
6. h
7. q
8. f
9. a
10. m
11. j
12. e
13. n
14. k
15. d
16. b
17. g
18. s
19. r
20. c

C. (p. 76)
1. inscribe
2. descriptive
3. intercept
4. recapture
5. tactile
6. receptor
7. circumscribe
8. description
9. postscript
10. contact
11. capture
12. interceptive
13. intact
14. receptive
15. describe
16. inscription
17. prescribe

18. prescription
19. interceptor
20. circumscriptive

D. (p. 77)
1. description
2. capture
3. receptive
4. inscription
5. intact
6. intercept
7. descriptive
8. receptor
9. describe
10. interceptive
11. contact
12. prescribe
13. tactile
14. prescription
15. recapture
16. inscribe
17. postscript
18. circumscribe
19. interceptor
20. circumscriptive

Lesson 13
A. (p. 79)
1. interrupt
2. contradict
3. rupture
4. prediction
5. corruption
6. contradiction
7. predict
8. corrupt
9. diction
10. interruption

B. (p. 80)
1. contradict
2. corruption
3. rupture
4. prediction
5. interrupt
6. predict
7. corrupt
8. interruption
9. diction
10. contradiction

C. (p. 81)
1. before, in front of
2. to break, burst
3. with, together
4. an action or process; state, quality, act
5. between, among

6. say, speak
7. state, quality, act; that which; process, condition
8. against, opposite

D. (p. 82)
Sentences will vary.

E. (p. 82)
Paragraphs will vary.

Lesson 14
A. (p. 83)
1. imposition
2. deposit
3. composition
4. opposition
5. expose
6. deposition
7. oppose
8. compose
9. exposition
10. impose

B. (p. 84)
1. expose
2. opposition
3. deposit
4. composition
5. imposition
6. compose
7. oppose
8. impose
9. deposition
10. exposition

C. (p. 85)
1. out, away, from
2. to, toward, against
3. an action or process; state, quality, act
4. with, together
5. place, put
6. from, away, down, apart; not
7. in, into; not

D. (p. 86)
Sentences will vary.

E. (p. 86)
Paragraphs will vary.

Review Lessons 13 and 14

A. (p. 87)

1. cor- or com-
2. pose/posit
3. -ion
4. com- or cor-
5. dict
6. rupt
7. -ure
8. de-
9. ex-
10. im-
11. op-
12. contra-
13. inter-
14. pre-

B. (p. 88)

1. h
2. o
3. s
4. r
5. l
6. m
7. p
8. a
9. q
10. t
11. n
12. e
13. f
14. k
15. b
16. g
17. i
18. d
19. c
20. j

C. (p. 89)

1. compose
2. predict
3. exposition
4. contradiction
5. impose
6. interruption
7. deposition
8. diction
9. oppose
10. corrupt
11. contradict
12. expose
13. prediction
14. composition
15. corruption
16. deposit
17. interrupt
18. imposition
19. rupture
20. opposition

D. (p. 90)

1. opposition
2. imposition
3. contradict
4. diction
5. contradiction
6. compose
7. prediction
8. rupture
9. expose
10. composition
11. Deposit
12. corruption
13. predict

14. interruption
15. interrupt
16. corrupt
17. oppose
18. impose
19. exposition
20. deposition

Lesson 15

A. (p. 92)

1. fragment
2. fracture
3. fragile
4. fraction
5. fragmental
6. fractional
7. fragility
8. infraction
9. fragmentary
10. fragmentation

B. (p. 93)

1. fraction
2. fragility
3. fragment
4. infraction
5. fracture
6. fragmentary
7. fragile
8. fragmental
9. fragmentation
10. fractional

C. (p. 94)

1. state, quality, act
2. an action or process
3. state, quality, act; that which; process, condition
4. that which, state, quality, act
5. an action or process; state, quality, act
6. like, of, relating to
7. like, related to; an action or process
8. that which; someone or something that belongs to; of, related to; one who
9. in, into; not
10. break

D. (p. 95)
Sentences will vary.

E. (p. 95)
Paragraphs will vary.

Lesson 16
A. (p. 96)
1. animate
2. equanimity
3. credence
4. incredible
5. incredulous
6. inanimate
7. credible
8. credulous
9. equity
10. equitable

B. (p. 97)
1. incredible
2. incredulous
3. equanimity
4. credence
5. animate
6. credulous
7. equity
8. equitable
9. credible
10. inanimate

C. (p. 98)
1. state, quality, act
2. equal, fair
3. to make, to act; one who, that which
4. in, into; not
5. believe
6. able to be
7. state, quality, act
8. able to be
9. spirit, life
10. having the quality of

D. (p. 99)
Sentences will vary.

E. (p. 99)
Paragraphs will vary.

Review Lessons 15 and 16
A. (p. 100)
1. in-
2. anim
3. -ate
4. cred
5. equ
6. -ence or -ity
   or il-ity
7. -ible or it-able
8. -ity or -ence
   or il-ity
9. -ulous
10. -ary
11. -ile
12. fract/frag
13. -ion
14. -ment
15. -ure
16. -al
17. il-ity or -ence
    or -ity
18. -ation
19. it-able or -ible

B. (p. 101)
1. q
2. s
3. p
4. k
5. n
6. r
7. o
8. m
9. l
10. t
11. d
12. i
13. h
14. e
15. g
16. c
17. a
18. f
19. b
20. j

C. (p. 102)
1. equitable
2. animate
3. fragmentary
4. fraction
5. credulous
6. equanimity
7. fragmentation
8. fracture
9. equity
10. credence
11. fragmental
12. infraction
13. credible
14. inanimate
15. fragility
16. fractional
17. fragile
18. incredible
19. fragment
20. incredulous

D. (p. 103)
1. equanimity
2. incredulous
3. infraction
4. fraction
5. equitable
6. fracture
7. equity
8. fragile
9. fragment
10. credible
11. credulous
12. fragmental
13. fractional
14. inanimate
15. credence
16. incredible
17. fragmentary
18. animate
19. fragility
20. fragmentation

Lesson 17
  A. (p. 105)
    1. deduct
    2. abduct
    3. induct
    4. benevolent
    5. volition
    6. deduction
    7. induction
    8. benevolence
    9. abduction
   10. deductive

  B. (p. 106)
    1. deduction
    2. benevolence
    3. abduction
    4. deductive
    5. benevolent
    6. deduct
    7. induction
    8. abduct
    9. induct
   10. volition

  C. (p. 107)
    1. tending to or performing
    2. in, into; not
    3. lead
    4. one who, that which; like, related to
    5. an action or process; state, quality, act
    6. away, from
    7. good, well
    8. will, wish
    9. state, quality, act
   10. from, away, down, apart; not
   11. state, quality, act

  D. (p. 108)
      Sentences will vary.

  E. (p. 108)
      Paragraphs will vary.

Lesson 18
  A. (p. 109)
    1. traverse
    2. extrovert
    3. introversion
    4. convert
    5. aversion
    6. introvert
    7. avert
    8. conversion
    9. extroversion
   10. invert

  B. (p. 110)
    1. traverse
    2. extrovert
    3. aversion
    4. convert
    5. introversion
    6. introvert
    7. avert
    8. conversion
    9. extroversion
   10. invert

  C. (p. 111)
    1. across, through
    2. in, into; not
    3. an action or process; state, quality, act
    4. within
    5. with, together
    6. turn
    7. away, from; not, without
    8. outside of

  D. (p. 112)
      Sentences will vary.

  E. (p. 112)
      Paragraphs will vary.

Review Lessons 17 and 18
  A. (p. 113)

1.	con-	11.	-ence or i-tion
2.	intro-	12.	-ive
3.	ab-	13.	i-tion or -ence
4.	duct	14.	extro-
5.	-ent	15.	vers/verse/
6.	bene-		vert
7.	de-	16.	in-
8.	a-	17.	tra-
9.	vol		
10.	-ion		

  B: (p. 114)

1.	k	11.	a
2.	o	12.	g
3.	p	13.	h
4.	s	14.	i
5.	q	15.	b
6.	t	16.	c
7.	l	17.	e
8.	m	18.	j
9.	n	19.	d
10.	r	20.	f

C. (p. 115)
1. aversion
2. invert
3. abduction
4. deductive
5. convert
6. extroversion
7. induct
8. benevolence
9. extrovert
10. conversion
11. benevolent
12. abduct
13. introversion
14. avert
15. volition
16. induction
17. deduct
18. traverse
19. introvert
20. deduction

D. (p. 116)
1. benevolent
2. deduction
3. volition
4. traverse
5. deduct
6. induction
7. extrovert
8. invert
9. deductive
10. abduct
11. benevolence
12. avert
13. aversion
14. convert
15. abduction
16. introversion
17. induct
18. conversion
19. introvert
20. extroversion

Lesson 19
A. (p. 118)
1. loquacious
2. misnomer
3. nominal
4. loquaciously
5. eloquent
6. nomination
7. eloquence
8. nominally
9. loquaciousness
10. eloquently

B. (p. 119)
1. loquaciously
2. misnomer
3. nominal
4. eloquent
5. loquacious
6. loquaciousness
7. nominally
8. nomination
9. eloquence
10. eloquently

C. (p. 120)
1. an action or process
2. out, away, from
3. speak
4. in the manner of; having the quality of
5. having the quality of
6. state, quality, act
7. name, law, custom, order
8. bad, wrong
9. like, related to; an action or process
10. state, quality, act
11. one who, that which
12. one who, that which; like, related to

D. (p. 121)
Sentences will vary.

E. (p. 121)
Paragraphs will vary.

Lesson 20
A. (p. 122)
1. carnivorous
2. voracious
3. manual
4. devour
5. manuscript
6. describe
7. description
8. inscribe
9. indescribable
10. inscription

B. (p. 123)
1. voracious
2. manual
3. carnivorous
4. devour
5. manuscript
6. Describe
7. inscription
8. indescribable
9. description
10. inscribe

C. (p. 124)
1. eat
2. able to be
3. from. away, down, apart; not
4. having the quality of
5. flesh, meat
6. in, into; not
7. like, related to; an action or process
8. having the quality of
9. write, written
10. hand
11. an action or process; state, quality, act

D. (p. 125)
Sentences will vary.

E. (p. 125)
Paragraphs will vary.

Review Lessons 19 and 20

A. (p. 126)
1. de-
2. carni
3. manu
4. scrib/scribe/ script
5. e-
6. mis-
7. loqu
8. nom/nomin
9. -ous or -acious
10. -al
11. -ence or -ness
12. -ent
13. -er
14. -ation
15. -ly
16. -ness or -ness
17. vor/vour
18. -acious or -ous
19. in-
20. -able
21. -ion

B. (p. 127)
1. l
2. o
3. n
4. m
5. t
6. q
7. j
8. p
9. s
10. g
11. r
12. a
13. d
14. c
15. b
16. h
17. f
18. k
19. i
20. e

C. (p. 128)
1. manual
2. indescribable
3. eloquent
4. nominally
5. manuscript
6. inscribe
7. nominal
8. loquaciously
9. carnivorous
10. inscription
11. misnomer

12. nomination
13. eloquence
14. loquaciousness
15. devour
16. describe
17. voracious
18. description
19. eloquently
20. loquacious

D. (p. 129)
1. voracious
2. loquaciously
3. misnomer
4. describe
5. eloquent
6. nomination
7. inscribe
8. description
9. nominally
10. indescribable
11. loquacious
12. nominal
13. eloquently
14. manual
15. manuscript
16. devour
17. loquaciousness
18. eloquence
19. inscription
20. carnivorous

Lesson 21

A. (p. 131)
1. unilateral
2. bicentennial
3. bilateral
4. centennial
5. perennial
6. lateral
7. annual
8. biannual
9. laterally
10. annually

B. (p. 132)
1. perennial
2. bicentennial
3. bilateral
4. unilateral
5. centennial
6. lateral
7. annual
8. laterally
9. biannual
10. annually

C. (p. 133)
1. like, related to; an action or process
2. hundred
3. side
4. two
5. in the manner of; having the quality of
6. one
7. through, very
8. year

D. (p. 134)
    Sentences will vary.

E. (p. 134)
    Paragraphs will vary.

Lesson 22
A. (p. 135)
1. temporary
2. contemporary
3. extemporaneous
4. veracity
5. temporal
6. contemporaneously
7. veritable
8. verification
9. extemporaneously
10. veracious

B. (p. 136)
1. extemporaneous
2. veracity
3. temporal
4. temporary
5. contemporary
6. veritable
7. contemporaneously
8. verification
9. extemporaneously
10. veracious

C. (p. 137)
1. time
2. able to be
3. the quality of
4. with, together
5. of, related to; an action or process
6. truth
7. in the manner of; having the quality of
8. an action or process
9. out, away, from
10. having the quality of
11. that which; someone or something that belongs to; of, related to; one who
12. having the quality of

D. (p. 138)
    Sentences will vary.

E. (p. 138)
    Paragraphs will vary.

Review Lessons 21 and 22
A. (p. 139)

1. bi-		10. -al
2. cent		11. con-
3. -ly		12. ex-
4. it-able		13. ific-ation
5. per-		14. tempor
6. uni-		15. ver
7. annu/enni		16. -acity
8. -acious		17. -aneous
9. later		18. -ary

B. (p. 140)

1. g		11. d
2. t		12. m
3. o		13. l
4. k		14. f
5. r		15. c
6. n		16. j
7. a		17. h
8. q		18. e
9. s		19. i
10. p		20. b

C. (p. 141)
1. verification
2. contemporary
3. annually
4. bicentennial
5. veracious
6. extemporaneous
7. biannual
8. centennial
9. extemporaneously
10. temporary
11. laterally
12. perennial
13. contemporaneously
14. veracity
15. annual
16. bilateral
17. temporal
18. veritable
19. unilateral
20. lateral

D. (p. 142)
1. centennial
2. temporary
3. veritable
4. lateral
5. annually
6. contemporaneously
7. temporal

8. verification
9. laterally
10. biannual
11. veracity
12. annual
13. extemporaneously
14. veracious
15. contemporary
16. perennial
17. unilateral
18. extemporaneous
19. bicentennial
20. bilateral

Lesson 23
A. (p. 144)
1. endure
2. vivid
3. revive
4. vivacious
5. durable
6. convivial
7. vividly
8. revival
9. duration
10. vivaciously

B. (p. 145)
1. vivid
2. durable
3. duration
4. revival
5. vivaciously
6. vividly
7. revive
8. vivacious
9. endure
10. convivial

C. (p. 146)
1. live, life
2. in the manner of, having the quality of
3. with, together
4. able to be
5. back, again
6. harden, to last, lasting
7. having the quality of
8. like, related to
9. like, related to; an action or process
10. an action or process
11. in, into

D. (p. 147)
Sentences will vary.

E. (p. 147)
Paragraphs will vary.

Lesson 24
A. (p. 148)
1. equate
2. exclaim
3. vocalize
4. equity
5. equivocate
6. equation
7. vocation
8. proclaim
9. exclamation
10. proclamation

B. (p. 149)
1. equity
2. proclamation
3. equivocate
4. proclaim
5. exclaim
6. equate
7. exclamation
8. equation
9. vocalize
10. vocation

C. (p. 150)
1. to make, to act
2. out, away, from
3. voice, call
4. for, before, forward
5. call out, shout
6. to make, to act; one who, that which
7. an action or process
8. equal, fair
9. state, quality, act
10. like, related to; an action or process

D. (p. 151)
Sentences will vary.

E. (p. 151)
Paragraphs will vary.

Review Lessons 23 and 24
A. (p. 152)
1. ex-
2. -en
3. pro-
4. claim/clam
5. -able
6. -acious
7. re-
8. dur/dure
9. viv/vive
10. -al/i-al
11. -ation
12. -id
13. equ/equi
14. voc
15. -ate
16. con-
17. -ize
18. -ity
19. -ly

B. (p. 153)

1. m	11. f
2. t	12. d
3. n	13. a
4. l	14. c
5. p	15. i
6. k	16. e
7. s	17. j
8. r	18. h
9. o	19. g
10. q	20. b

C. (p. 154)
1. equivocate
2. vocation
3. revive
4. durable
5. vividly
6. exclaim
7. proclamation
8. equation
9. vocalize
10. endure
11. convivial
12. duration
13. equity
14. exclamation
15. vivaciously
16. revival
17. proclaim
18. equate
19. vivid
20. vivacious

D. (p. 155)
1. equate
2. vocation
3. durable
4. revive
5. endure
6. exclaim
7. equation
8. proclaim
9. convivial
10. vivaciously
11. duration
12. equivocate
13. exclamation
14. vocalize
15. vivid
16. revival
17. equity
18. vividly
19. proclamation
20. vivacious

Lesson 25

A. (p. 157)
1. cumulative
2. illuminate
3. accumulate
4. luminous
5. luminary
6. cumulus
7. illuminative
8. luminosity
9. luminescent
10. illumination

B. (p. 158)
1. luminous
2. cumulative
3. accumulate
4. luminary
5. illuminate
6. illuminative
7. cumulus
8. luminosity
9. illumination
10. luminescent

C. (p. 159)
1. thing which
2. mass, heap
3. in, into; not
4. an action or process
5. state, quality, act
6. light
7. that which; someone or something that belongs to; related to; one who
8. to, toward, near
9. to make, to act; one who, that which
10. tending to or performing
11. having the quality of
12. becoming, having

D. (p. 160)
   Sentences will vary.

E. (p. 160)
   Paragraphs will vary.

Lesson 26

A. (p. 161)
1. renovate
2. vociferous
3. innovation
4. novice
5. revocable
6. novelist
7. innovate
8. irrevocable
9. renovation
10. novelty

B. (p. 162)
1. revocable
2. renovate
3. innovation
4. vociferous
5. novice
6. innovate
7. renovation
8. irrevocable
9. novelty
10. novelist

C. (p. 163)
1. one who
2. back, again
3. new
4. able to be
5. in, into; not
6. to make, to act; one who, that which
7. voice, call
8. an action or process
9. in, into; not
10. producing
11. state, quality, that which
12. one who, that which

D. (p. 164)
Sentences will vary.

E. (p. 164)
Paragraphs will vary.

Review Lessons 25 and 26
A. (p. 165)
1. ac-
2. lumin
3. -ate
4. at-ive
5. -ous
6. ir- or il- or in-
7. re-
8. nov
9. voc/voci
10. -able
11. in- or ir- or il-
12. el-ist
13. el-ty
14. -ation
15. -ferous
16. -ice
17. il- or in- or ir-
18. cumul
19. os-ity
20. -us
21. -escent
22. -ary

B. (p. 166)
1. l
2. p
3. q
4. t
5. r
6. o
7. n
8. m
9. s
10. k
11. j
12. a
13. h
14. g
15. f
16. b
17. c
18. e
19. i
20. d

C. (p. 167)
1. illuminative
2. novelist
3. innovation
4. accumulate
5. novelty
6. cumulative
7. illumination
8. novice
9. irrevocable
10. renovate
11. illuminate
12. luminescent
13. revocable
14. innovate
15. vociferous
16. luminary
17. cumulus
18. luminous
19. renovation
20. luminosity

D. (p. 168)
1. cumulative
2. novice
3. innovation
4. accumulate
5. revocable
6. renovate
7. vociferous
8. illuminate
9. cumulus
10. luminosity
11. innovate
12. irrevocable
13. novelty
14. renovation
15. luminary
16. illuminative
17. luminous
18. novelist
19. illumination
20. luminescent

Lesson 27
A. (p. 170)
1. herbivorous
2. conclusion
3. seclude
4. exclusion
5. herbicide
6. conclude
7. exclusive
8. conclusive
9. exclude
10. seclusion

B. (p. 171)
1. exclusion
2. seclude
3. herbicide
4. conclusion
5. herbivorous
6. seclusion
7. conclude
8. exclusive
9. exclude
10. conclusive

C. (p. 172)
1. kill
2. with, together
3. grass
4. apart, aside
5. an action or process; state, quality, act
6. close
7. out, away, from
8. eat
9. tending to or performing
10. having the quality of

D. (p. 173)
Sentences will vary.

E. (p. 173)
Paragraphs will vary.

Lesson 28
A. (p. 174)
1. contortion
2. unison
3. dissonance
4. distort
5. ultrasonic
6. contort
7. dissonant
8. formation
9. distortion
10. uniform

B. (p. 175)
1. dissonant
2. uniform
3. contort
4. distortion
5. formation
6. contortion
7. ultrasonic
8. distort
9. unison
10. dissonance

C. (p. 176)
1. apart, opposite of
2. one who, that which; state, quality
3. sound
4. an action or process
5. like, related to
6. with, together
7. state, quality, act
8. beyond
9. twist
10. shape, form
11. one
12. an action or process; state, quality, act

D. (p. 177)
Sentences will vary.

E. (p. 177)
Paragraphs will vary.

Review Lessons 27 and 28
A. (p. 178)

1. ultra-		11. ex-	
2. uni-		12. se-	
3. son		13. clude/clus	
4. tort		14. herbi	
5. -ance		15. vor	
6. -ive		16. -cide	
7. -ion		17. -ation	
8. con-		18. -ous	
9. dis-		19. form	
10. -ic		20. -ant	

B. (p. 179)

1. r		11. g	
2. s		12. i	
3. p		13. h	
4. t		14. j	
5. o		15. e	
6. q		16. c	
7. k		17. f	
8. m		18. a	
9. l		19. b	
10. n		20. d	

C. (p. 180)
1. seclusion
2. formation
3. exclude
4. distort
5. conclusive
6. contortion
7. exclusive
8. unison
9. conclude
10. ultrasonic
11. herbivorous

12. dissonance
13. seclude
14. distortion
15. exclusion
16. dissonant
17. herbicide
18. uniform
19. contort
20. conclusion

D. (p. 181)
1. ultrasonic
2. contortion
3. conclusion
4. Herbivorous
5. conclude
6. contort
7. formation
8. exclusion
9. dissonant
10. distort
11. seclude
12. herbicide
13. exclusive
14. distortion
15. unison
16. conclusive
17. uniform
18. dissonance
19. seclusion
20. exclude

Lesson 29
A. (p. 183)
1. envision
2. invisible
3. specify
4. retrospect
5. inspection
6. inspect
7. visible
8. retrospective
9. specification
10. retrospection

B. (p. 184)
1. envision
2. inspection
3. specify
4. invisible
5. retrospect
6. inspect
7. specification
8. retrospective
9. visible
10. retrospection

C. (p. 185)
1. to make, to act, to do
2. in, into
3. see
4. an action or process
5. in, into; not
6. able to be
7. look, examine
8. backward
9. an action or process; state, quality, act
10. tending to or performing

D. (p. 186)
Sentences will vary.

E. (p. 186)
Paragraphs will vary.

Lesson 30
A. (p. 187)
1. admit
2. dissect
3. intermission
4. remittance
5. admission
6. intersection
7. emissary
8. remit
9. intersect
10. dissection

B. (p. 188)
1. intersect
2. intersection
3. remit
4. emissary
5. admit
6. dissection
7. intermission
8. dissect
9. remittance
10. Admission

C. (p. 189)
1. that which; someone or something that belongs to; of, related to, one who
2. out, away, from
3. between, among
4. cut
5. to, toward, near
6. send, let go
7. state, quality, act
8. an action or process; state, quality, act
9. back, again
10. apart, opposite of

D. (p. 190)
Sentences will vary.

E. (p. 190)

    Paragraphs will vary.

Review Lessons 29 and 30

A. (p. 191)

1. ad-	11. -ion
2. sect	12. -ive
3. -ance	13. dis-
4. en-	14. e-
5. spec/spect	15. inter-
6. -ible	16. re-
7. in-	17. -ary
8. retro-	18. ific-ation
9. vis	19. miss/mit/mitt
10. i-fy	

B. (p. 192)

1. p	11. i
2. r	12. c
3. l	13. h
4. q	14. j
5. o	15. e
6. s	16. a
7. t	17. d
8. m	18. b
9. k	19. f
10. n	20. g

C. (p. 193)

1. dissection
2. admit
3. inspection
4. retrospective
5. intersect
6. emissary
7. retrospect
8. specification
9. remittance
10. admission
11. retrospection
12. specify
13. envision
14. invisible
15. remit
16. dissect
17. intersection
18. visible
19. intermission
20. inspect

D. (p. 194)

1. retrospect
2. remit
3. specify
4. Admission
5. intersect
6. emissary

7. visible
8. intermission
9. specification
10. envision
11. invisible
12. remittance
13. inspection
14. admit
15. dissect
16. inspect
17. intersection
18. dissection
19. retrospection
20. retrospective

Dictionary

Pronunciation Key

ă	asp, fat	ə	a in ago	
ā	ape, date, play		e in agent	
ĕ	elf, ten, berry		i in sanity	
ē	even, meet, money		o in comply	
ĭ	is, hit, mirror		u in focus	
ī	ice, bite, high	ər	perhaps, murder	
ŏ	ah, car, father			
ō	open, tone, go	sh	she, cushion, dash	
ô	all, horn, law	th	thin, nothing, truth	
o͞o	ooze, tool, crew	*th*	then, father, lathe	
oo	look, pull, moor	*zh*	azure, leisure	
yo͞o	use, cute, few			
yoo	united, cure, globule	'	primary accent	
ŭ	up, cut, color	'	secondary accent	
ûr	urn, fur, deter			

Latin Prefixes

a- away, from; not, without

aversion: the act of turning away from; a dislike of something [ə-vûr'-zhən]

avert: to turn away; to keep from happening [ə-vûrt']

ab- away, from

abbreviate: to shorten [ə-brē'vē-āt']

abduct: to take away by force [əb-dŭkt']

abduction: a taking away by force [əb-dŭk'-shən]

ac- to, toward, near

accede: to agree; to yield to [ək-sēd]

accelerate: to increase the speed of [ək-sĕl'-ə-rāt']

acceleration: the action or process of increasing the speed of [ək-sĕl'-ə-rā'-shən]

accessible: easily entered, approached, or obtained [ək-sĕs'-ə-bəl]

accumulate: to gather or pile up little by little [ə-kyo͞om'-yə-lāt']

ad- to, toward, near

admission: entry; entrance fee [əd-mĭ'-shən]

admit: let enter, give access to [əd-mĭt']

bene- good, well

benevolence: the act of doing good; kindliness [bə-nĕv'-ə-lənts]

benevolent: showing kindness or goodwill [bə-nĕv'-ə-lənt]

bi- two

biannual: happening twice a year [bī-ăn'-yoo-əl]

bicentennial: of or relating to an age or period of 200 years [bī'-sĕn-tĕn'-ē-əl]

bilateral: of or involving two sides; reciprocal [bī-lăt'-ər-əl]

cent- hundred

centennial: of or relating to an age or period of 100 years [sĕn-tĕn'-ē-əl]

circum- around

circumscribe: to draw around; to encircle [sûr'-kəm-skrīb']

circumscriptive: tending to limit or enclose; restrictive [sûr'-kəm-skrĭp'-tĭv]

circumvent: to go around; to bypass restrictions [sûr'-kəm-vĕnt']

circumvention: process of going around; the act of bypassing restrictions [sûr'-kəm-vĕn'-chən]

circumventive: tending to go around; tending to bypass restrictions [sûr'-kəm-vĕn'tiv]

com- with, together

commemorate: to honor the memory of, as by a ceremony [kə-měm'-ə-rāt']

commotion: the scene of noisy confusion or activity [kə-mō'-shən]

compose: to put together or arrange in proper order [kəm-pōz']

composition: an arrangement or putting together of parts [kŏm'-pə-zĭsh'-ən]

con- with, together

conclude: to bring to a close; end; finish [kən-klo͞od']

conclusion: the end or last part [kən-klo͞o'-zhən]

conclusive: that which settles a question; decisive; final [kən-klo͞o'-siv]

construct: to form by putting together parts [kən-strŭkt']

construction: the action or process of building [kən-strŭkt'-shən]

contact: the state of touching or meeting [kŏn'-tăkt']

contemporaneously: having the quality of existing, occurring, or originating at the same time [kən-těm'-pə-rā'-nē-əs-lē]

contemporary: of the same time; modern time [kən-těm'-pə-rěr'-ē]

contort: to twist from its usual shape or position [kən-tôrt']

contortion: a twisted shape or position [kən-tôr'-shən]

contract: to draw together [kən-trăkt]

contraction: act of drawing together or shrinking [kən-trăk'-shən]

convene: to meet together; assemble [kən-vēn]

convent: religious house where a community of nuns reside [kŏn'-vənt]

convention: a gathering or assembly of people with a common interest [kən-věn'-chən]

conversion: a change from one thing, state, or religion to another [kən-vûr'-zhən]

convert: to turn into or transform [kən-vûrt']

convince: to persuade by argument or evidence [kən-vĭns']

convincible: able to be conquered; able to be made to agree with [kən-vĭn'-sə-bəl]

convivial: lively, jovial, friendly [kən-vĭv'-ē-əl]

contra- against, opposite

contradict: to express or imply the opposite of [kŏn'-trə-dĭkt']

contradiction: an action in opposition to another [kŏn'-trə-dĭk'-shən]

cor- with, together

corrupt: to cause to break with what is legally or morally right [kuh-rupt']

corruption: a break with what is legally or morally right [kuh-rup'-shən]

counter- against, opposite

counteract: to act directly against; to prevent from affecting [koun'-tər-ăkt']

de- from, away, down; apart; not

decelerate: to reduce the speed of [dē-sĕl'-ə-rāt']

deceleration: the action or process of reducing the speed of [dē-sĕl'-ə-rā'-shən]

deduct: to subtract; to take away [dĭ-dŭkt']

deduction: a subtraction of an amount [dĭ-dŭk'-shən]

deductive: tending to use logic or reason to form a conclusion [dĭ-dŭk'-tĭv]

deposit: to put down or in a safe place [dĭ-pŏz'-ĭt]

deposition: the act of putting down or depositing; the removing from power [dĕ-pə-zi'-shən]

describe: to represent with words or pictures [dĭ-skrīb']

description: action or process of picturing in words [də-skrĭp'-shən]

descriptive: tending to put forth in words [də-skrĭp'-tĭv]

destruct: to deliberately destroy an object [dĭ-strŭkt']

destruction: the act of destroying; a state of damage [dĭ-strŭk'-shən]

determination: an intent to reach a goal [dĭ-tûr'-mə-nā'-shən]

devour: to eat quickly [dĭ-vour']

indescribable: not able to be described [in-də-skrīb'-ə-bəl]

di- apart, away; not

digress: to depart from the main issue, subject, etc. [dī-grĕs']

digression: a departure from the main issue, subject, etc. [dī-grĕsh'ən]

dis-   apart, opposite of

dissect: to cut apart piece by piece [dĭ-sĕkt']

dissection: an analysis part by part, a detailed examination [dĭ-sĕk'-shən]

dissonance: lack of harmony; discord [dĭs'-ə-nəns]

dissonant: charcterized by a lack of harmony; discordant [dĭs'-ə-nənt]

distort: to alter the shape or condition of [dĭ-stôrt']

distortion: the process of altering the shape or condition of [dĭ-stôr'-shən]

e-   out, away, from

eloquence: speech that is vivid, fluent, forceful, and graceful [ĕl'-ə-kwənts]

eloquent: speaking beautifully and forcefully [ĕl'-ə-kwənt]

eloquently: speaking in a vivid, fluent, forceful, and graceful manner [ĕl'-ə-kwənt-lē]

emissary: a representative of a country or group sent on a mission [ĕm'-ĭ-sĕr'-ē]

en-   in, into

endure: to remain, to last [ĕn-door]

envision: to picture in the mind [ĕn-vĭzh'-ən]

ex-   out, away, from

exclaim: to cry out or speak in a strong or sudden manner [ĭk-sklām']

exclamation: an outcry, a shout [ĕk'-sklə-mā'-shən]

exclude: to shut or rule out; to refuse to admit or include [ĭk-sklood']

exclusion: a shutting out; rejection [ĭk-skloo'-zhən]

exclusive: shutting or ruling out other options, tending to shut out others [ĭk-skloo'-siv]

expose: to place something where it can be seen; to put in an unprotected situation [ĭk-spōz']

exposition: a writing or speaking that puts forth or explains [ĕk'-spə-zish'-ən]

extemporaneous: done without any preparation; impromptu [ĭk-stĕm'-pə-rā'-nē-əs]

extemporaneously: in a spur of the moment manner [ĭk-stĕm'-pə-rā'-nē-əs-lē]

exterminate: to destroy or get rid of completely [ĭk-stûr'-mə-nāt']

extermination: process of destroying or getting rid of completely [ĭk-stûr'-mə-nā'-shən]

extract: to pull or draw out from [ĭk-străkt']

extractible: able to be pulled or drawn out from [ĭk-străk'-tə-bəl]

extraction: process of withdrawing, pulling out [ĭk-străk'-shən]

extro-   outside of

extroversion: turning outward; focusing on others [ĕk'-strə-vûr'-zhən]

extrovert: an outgoing person [ĕk'-strə-vûrt']

il-   in, into; not

illuminate: to give light to [ĭ-loo'-mə-nāt']

illumination: the process of lighting up [ĭ-loo'-mə-nā'-shən]

illuminative: tending to produce light [ĭ-loo'-mə-nə-tĭv]

im-   in, into; not

immobile: motionless; unable to move [ĭ-mō'-bəl]

immobility: relating to the quality of not being able to move [ĭm-ō-bĭl'-ə-tē]

immovable: unable to move or be moved; fixed; immobile [ĭ-moo'-və-bəl]

impose: to put an excessive or unjust burden on someone [ĭm-pōz']

imposition: an excessive or unjust burden placed on someone [ĭm'-pə-zĭsh'-ən]

in-   in, into; not

inaction: the state of not doing something that should be done; idleness [ĭ-năk'-shən]

inanimate: not filled with life or spirit; motionless [ĭ-nă'-nə-mət]

inaudible: unable to be heard [ĭn-ô'-də-bəl]

incredible: too extraordinary and impossible to believe [ĭn-krĕd'-ə-bəl]

incredulous: disbelieving; not believing [ĭn-krĕj'-ə-ləs]

indescribable: not able to be described [ĭn-də-skrī'-bə-bəl]

induct: to formally install someone to an office or position [ĭn-dŭkt']

induction: the process of formally installing someone to an office or position [ĭn-dŭk'-shən]

infraction: the act of breaking the limits or rules [ĭn-frăk'-shən]

innovate: to introduce new methods, devices, etc. [ĭn'-ə-vāt']

innovation: a new idea, method, or device [ĭn'-ə-vā'-shən]

inscribe: to write or engrave on some surface [ĭn-skrīb']

inscription: an engraving on a coin or other object [ĭn-skrĭp'-shən]

inspect: to examine, to look over carefully [ĭn-spĕkt']

inspection: the act of examining or reviewing [ĭn-spĕk'-shən]

intact: with nothing missing; left whole [ĭn-tăkt']

invert: to turn inside out or upside down [ĭn-vûrt']

invincible: unbeatable; impossible to overcome [ĭn-vĭn'-sə-bəl]

invisible: impossible to see [ĭn-vĭz'-ə-bəl]

infra-　beneath

infrastructure: underlying framework of a system [ĭn'-frə-strŭk'-chər]

inter-　between, among

interact: to talk or do things with others [ĭn-tər-ăkt']

interaction: communication between two or more things [ĭn'-tər-ăk'-shən]

intercept: to stop or interrupt the course of [ĭn'-tər-sĕpt']

interceptive: tending to stop or interrupt the course of [ĭn'-tər-sĕp'-tĭv]

interceptor: a person or thing that stops or interrupts the course of [ĭn'-tər-sĕp'-tər]

intermission: interval of time between periods of activity; a pause [ĭn'-tər-mĭ'-shən]

interrupt: to stop or hinder by breaking in on [ĭn'-tə-rŭpt']

interruption: action of stopping or hindering by breaking in on [ĭn'-tə-rŭp'-shən]

intersect: to cut across, traverse [ĭn'-tər-sĕkt']

intersection: the place or point where two things cross each other [ĭn'-tər-sĕk'-shən]

intervene: to come between; to intercede [ĭn'-tər-vēn']

intervention: the action of coming between; act of interceding [ĭn'-tər-vĕn'-chən]

intro-　within

introversion: turning inward; focusing on oneself [ĭn'-trə-vûr'-zhən]

introvert: a person whose interest is more in himself than in others [ĭn'-trə-vûrt']

ir-　in, into; not

irrevocable: not subject to reversal [ĭ-rĕ'-və-kə-bəl]

mis-　bad, wrong

misnomer: an error in naming a person or thing [mĭs-nō'-mər]

ob-　to, toward, against

obstruct: to block or fill with obstacles [əb-strŭkt']

obstruction: an obstacle or something put up against something else [əb-strŭk'-shən]

op-　to, toward, against

oppose: to act in opposition to; to put against [ə-pōz']

opposition: the act of resistance or action against [ŏp'-ə-zĭsh'-ən]

per-　through, very

perennial: lasting through many years [pə-rĕn'-ē-əl]

post-　after

postscript: an addition to an already completed letter, article, or book [pōst'-skrĭpt']

pre-　before, in front of

predict: to tell or state a future event; foretell [prĭ-dĭkt']

prediction: a statement foretelling the future [prĭ-dĭk'-shən]

prescribe: to write or set down as a rule, order, or direction; to order or advise as a medicine [prĭ-skrīb']

prescription: a written order for medicine [prĭ-skrĭp'-shən]

pro-　for, before, forward

proceed: to go forward, especially after stopping [prō-sēd']

process: a method of doing or producing something [prŏ'-sĕs]

processable: able to be subjected to a series of actions that yield a change [prŏ'-sĕ-sə-bəl]

procession: the act of going forward in an orderly manner [prə-sě'-shən]

proclaim: to announce, to declare, to make public [prə-klām']

proclamation: something announced officially in public [prŏk'-lə-mā'-shən]

progress: movement forward or onward; improvement [prŏg'-rěs']

progression: the process or action of moving forward [prə-grě'-shən]

promote: to move forward or raise to a higher rank, class, status, etc. [prə-mōt']

promotion: an advancement in rank or position [prə-mō'-shən]

re-   back, again

irrevocable: not subject to reversal [ĭ-rě'-və-kə-bəl]

react: to act in return or reciprocally [rē-ăkt']

reaction: a response [rē-ăk'-shən]

recapture: the taking back of something [rē-kăp'-chər]

receptive: tending to receive; take in, admit, contain [rə-sěp'-tĭv]

receptor: that which holds or receives (in various senses) [rə-sěp'-tər]

recognition: act of acknowledging or noticing [rě'-kĭg-nĭsh'-ən]

recognize: to identify someone or something seen before [rěk'-əg-nīz']

reconstruct: to put back together again [rē'-kən-strŭkt']

reconstruction: the act of putting back together [rē'-kən-strŭk'-shən]

regress: to go back to an earlier state [rē-grěs']

regression: a movement backward to an earlier state [rĭ-grěsh'-ən]

rejuvenate: to bring back to youthful strength or appearance [rĭ-jōō'-və-nāt']

remit: discharge; pardon; set free, release [rə-mĭt']

remittance: the act of sending back money to pay [rĭ-mĭt'-ns]

removable: able to be taken or carried away [rĭ-mōō'-və-bəl]

renovate: to make something like new again [rěn'-ə-vāt']

renovation: the action or process of making something like new again [rěn'-ə-vā'-shən]

repugnant: distasteful; offensive or revolting [rĭ-pŭg'-nənt]

retract: to draw or pull back [rĭ-trăkt']

retraction: process of pulling back [rək-trăk'-shən]

revival: the act of bringing back to life; renewed interest in [rĭ-vī'-vəl]

revive: to bring back to life or consciousness [rə-vīv']

revocable: able to be repealed or withdrawn [rěv'-ə-kə-bəl]

retro-   backward

retrospect: the remembering of past events [rět'-rə-spěkt']

retrospection: the act of looking back on past events, experiences, etc. [rě'-trə-spěk'-shən]

retrospective: looking back on the past or past events [rě'-trə-spěk'-tĭv]

se-   apart, aside

secede: to formally break away from [sĭ-sēd']

secession: the act of formally withdrawing from a group [sĭ-sě'-shən]

seclude: to keep away from; to isolate [sĭ-klōōd']

seclusion: isolation; a shutting off or keeping away from others [sĭ-klōō'-zhən]

sub-   under, below

submarine: being, living, or used under water [sŭb'-mə-rēn']

tra-   across, through

traverse: to move across or turn back and forth across [trə-vurs']

ultra-   beyond

ultrasonic: related to a frequency of sound vibrations beyond the normal hearing range; high in frequency [ŭl'-trə-sŏn'-ĭk]

uni-   one

uniform: equal, at one, consistent [yoo'-nə-fôrm']

unilateral: affecting one side of something [yoo'-nə-lăt'-ər-əl]

unison: as one voice [yoo'-nĭ-sən]

Latin Roots

act   to do, to drive

counteract: to act directly against; to prevent from affecting [koun'-tər-ăkt']

inaction: the state of not doing something that should be done; idleness [ĭ-năk'-shən]

interact: to talk or do things with others [ĭn-tər-ăkt']

interaction: communication between two or more things [ĭn'-tər-ăk'-shən]

react: to act in return or reciprocally [rē-ăkt']

reaction: a response [rē-ăk'-shən]

anim   spirit, life

animate: to give spirit, life, motion, or activity to [ăn'-ə-māt']

equanimity: calm temperament; evenness of temper [ĕ'-kwə-nĭm'-ĭ-tē]

inanimate: not filled with life or spirit; motionless [ĭ-nă'-nə-mət]

annu   year

annual: related to a period of one year [ăn'-yoo-əl]

annually: in the manner of occurring once a year [ăn'-yoo-ə-lē]

biannual: happening twice a year [bī-ăn'-yoo-əl]

aqu   water

aquarium: a place where aquatic organisms are kept and exhibited [ə-kwĕr'-ē-əm]

aqueous: like, or having the quality of water; water [ā'-kwē-əs]

aqua   water

aquamarine: blue-green in color, like sea water [ŏk'-wə-mə-rēn']

aquatic: related to the animals and plants that live in or near water [ə-kwŏt'-ĭk]

aud   hear

audible: able to be heard [ô'-də-bəl]

audience: a group of listeners or spectators [ô'-dē-əns]

inaudible: unable to be heard [ĭn-ô'-də-bəl]

avi   bird

aviary: a large enclosure in which birds are kept [ā'-vē-ĕr'-ē]

aviator: one who flies an airplane; pilot [ā'-vē-ā'-tər]

avia   bird

aviation: the act or practice of flying airplanes, helicopters, etc. [ā'-vē-ā'-shən]

aviatrix: a woman airplane pilot [ā'-vē-ā'-trĭks]

brev   short

abbreviate: to shorten [ə-brē'-vē-āt']

brevity: quality of being brief; shortness in time [brĕv'-ĭ-tē]

capt   take, hold

capture: the act of taking or being taken by force [kăp'-chər]

recapture: the taking back of something [rē-kăp'-chər]

carni   flesh, meat

carnivorous: flesh-eating [kŏr-nĭv'-ər-əs]

cede   go, yield

accede: to agree; to yield to [ək-sēd]

secede: to formally break away from [sĭ-sēd']

ceed   go, yield

proceed: to go forward, especially after stopping [prō-sēd']

celer   fast

accelerate: to increase the speed of [ək-sĕl'-ə-rāt']

acceleration: the action or process of increasing the speed of [ək-sĕl'-ə-rā'-shən]

decelerate: to reduce the speed of [dē-sĕl'-ə-rāt']

deceleration: the action or process of reducing the speed of [dē-sĕl'-ə-rā'-shən]

cept   take, hold

intercept: to stop or interrupt the course of [ĭn'-tər-sĕpt']

interceptive: tending to stop or interrupt the course of [ĭn'-tər-sĕp'-tĭv]

interceptor: a person or thing that stops or interrupts the course of [ĭn'-tər-sĕp'-tər]

receptive: tending to receive; take in, admit, contain [rə-sĕp'-tĭv]

receptor: that which holds or receives (in various senses) [rə-sĕp'-tər]

cess   go, yield
accessible: easily entered, approached, or obtained [ək-sĕs'-ə-bəl]
process: a method of doing or producing something [prŏ'-sĕs]
processable: able to be subjected to a series of actions that yield a change [prŏ'-sĕ-sə-bəl]
procession: the act of going forward in an orderly manner [prə-sĕ'-shən]
secession: the act of formally withdrawing from a group [sĭ-sĕ'-shən]

claim   call out, shout
exclaim: to cry out or speak in a strong or sudden manner [ĭk-sklām']
proclaim: to announce, to declare, to make public [prə-klām']

clam   call out, shout
exclamation: an outcry, a shout [ĕk'-sklə-mā'-shən]
proclamation: something announced officially in public [prŏk'-lə-mā'-shən]

clude   close
conclude: to bring to a close; end; finish [kən-klo͞od']
exclude: to shut or rule out; to refuse to admit or include [ĭk-sklo͞od']
seclude: to keep away from; to isolate [sĭ-klo͞od']

clus   close
conclusion: the end or last part [kən-klo͞o'-zhən]
conclusive: that which settles a question; decisive; final [kən-klo͞o'-siv]
exclusion: a shutting out; rejection [ĭk-sklo͞o'-zhən]
exclusive: shutting or ruling out other options, tending to shut out others [ĭk-sklo͞o'-siv]
seclusion: isolation; a shutting off or keeping away from others [sĭ-klo͞o'-zhən]

cogn   know
cognition: process of acquiring knowledge [kŏg-nĭsh'-ən]
cognitive: having intellectual activity, as in thinking and reasoning [kŏg'-nə-tĭv]
cognizant: the state of being aware or informed of something [kŏg'-nə-zənt]
recognition: act of acknowledging or noticing [rĕ'-kĭg-nĭsh'-ən]
recognize: to identify someone or something seen before [rĕk'-əg-nīz']

cred   believe
credence: belief; acceptance as true or valid [krēd'-n(t)s]
credible: able to be believed; believable; reliable [krĕd'-ə-bəl]
credulous: believing too readily; gullible [krĕj'-ə-ləs]
incredible: too extraordinary and impossible to believe [ĭn-krĕd'-ə-bəl]
incredulous: disbelieving; not believing [ĭn-krĕj'-ə-ləs]

cumul   mass, heap
accumulate: to gather or pile up little by little [ə-kyo͞om'-yə-lāt']
cumulative: gradually building up [kyo͞om'-yə-lə-tĭv]
cumulus: a heap, a pile, a mass; a thick, puffy type of cloud [kyo͞om'-yə-ləs]

dict   say, speak
contradict: to express or imply the opposite of [kŏn'-trə-dĭkt']
contradiction: an action in opposition to another [kŏn'-trə-dĭk'-shən]
diction: the act or manner of expression in words [dĭk'-shən]
predict: to tell or state a future event; foretell [prĭ-dĭkt']
prediction: a statement foretelling the future [prĭ-dĭk'-shən]

duct   lead
abduct: to take away by force [əb-dŭkt']
abduction: a taking away by force [əb-dŭk'-shən]
deduct: to subtract; to take away [dĭ-dŭkt']
deduction: a subtraction of an amount [dĭ-dŭk'-shən]
deductive: tending to use logic or reason to form a conclusion [dĭ-dŭk'-tĭv]
induct: to formally install someone to an office or position [ĭn-dŭkt']
induction: the process of formally installing someone to an office or position [ĭn-dŭk'-shən]

dur   harden, to last, lasting
durable: having the quality of lasting [door'-ə-bəl]
duration: the length of time something lasts [doo-rā'-shən]

dure   harden, to last, lasting
endure: to remain, to last [ĕn-door]

enni   year

bicentennial: of or relating to an age or period of 200 years [bī-sĕn-tĕn′-ē-əl]

centennial: of or relating to an age or period of 100 years [sĕn-tĕn′-ē-əl]

perennial: lasting through many years [pə-rĕn′-ē-əl]

equ   equal, fair

equanimity: calm temperament, evenness of temper [ē′-kwə-nĭm′-ə-tē]

equate: to make, treat, or regard as equal or equivalent [ē-kwāt′]

equation: a statement of equality [ĭ-kwā′-zhən]

equitable: fair; just [ĕk′-wĭ-tə-bəl]

equity: fairness; the state of being just or fair [ĕk′-wĭ-tē]

equi   (combining form) equal, fair

equivocate: to use misleading language that could be interpreted two different ways [ĭ-kwĭv′-ə-kāt′]

form   shape, form

formation: process of shaping, forming, or establishing [fôr-mā′-shən]

uniform: equal, at one, consistent [yoo′-nə-fôrm′]

fract   break

fraction: a part or element of a larger whole [frăk′-shən]

fractional: related to being very small; insignificant [frăk′-shən-əl]

fracture: a break, crack, or split [frăk′-chər]

infraction: the act of breaking the limits or rules [ĭn-frăk′-shən]

frag   break

fragile: easily broken; delicate [frăj′-əl]

fragility: state of delicateness [frə-jĭl′-ə-tē]

fragment: a broken piece [frăg′-mənt]

fragmental: related to being incomplete or broken [frăg-mĕnt′-əl]

fragmentary: not complete; disconnected [frăg′-mən-tĕr′-ē]

fragmentation: process of breaking, cracking, or splitting; that which is broken or divided [frăg′-mən-tā′-shən]

gress   step

digress: to depart from the main issue, subject, etc. [dī-grĕs′]

digression: a departure from the main issue, subject, etc. [dī-grĕsh′-ən]

progress: movement forward or onward; improvement [prŏg′-rĕs′]

progression: the process or action of moving forward [prə-grĕ′-shən]

regress: to go back to an earlier state [rē-grĕs′]

regression: a movement backward to an earlier state [rĭ-grĕsh′-ən]

herbi   grass

herbicide: any chemical used to kill unwanted plants, etc. [hûr′-bĭ-sīd′]

herbivorous: plant-eating [hûr-bĭv′-ər-əs]

juven   young

juvenile: youthful or childish; immature [joo′-və-nīl′]

rejuvenate: to bring back to youthful strength or appearance [rĭ-joo′-və-nāt′]

later   side

bilateral: of or involving two sides; reciprocal [bī-lăt′-ər-əl]

lateral: of or relating to the side [lăt′-ər-əl]

laterally: by, to, or from the side; sideways [lăt′-ər-ə-lē]

unilateral: affecting one side of something [yoo′-nə-lăt′-ər-əl]

loqu   speak

eloquence: speech that is vivid, fluent, forceful, and graceful [ĕl′-ə-kwənts]

eloquent: speaking beautifully and forcefully [ĕl′-ə-kwənt]

eloquently: speaking in a vivid, fluent, forceful, and graceful manner [ĕl′-ə-kwənt-lē]

loquacious: very talkative [lō-kwā′-shəs]

loquaciously: in a very talkative or wordy manner [lō-kwā′-shəs-lē]

loquaciousness: the quality of being very talkative [lō-kwā′-shəs-nəs]

lumin   light

illuminate: to give light to [ĭ-loo′-mə-nāt′]

illumination: the process of lighting up [ĭ-loo′-mə-nā′-shən]

illuminative: tending to produce light [ĭ-loo′-mə-nə-tĭv]

luminary: an object, like a star, that gives off light; a famous person (a "star") [loo′-mə-nĕr′-ē]

luminescent: glowing, luminous
[lōō'-mə-něs'-ənt]
luminosity: the relative quantity of
light; a state of being luminous
[lōō'-mə-nŏs'-ə-tē]
luminous: giving off or reflecting light
[lōō'-mə-nəs]

manu   hand
manual: having to do with the hands
[măn'-yōō-əl]
manuscript: a handwritten document
or author's original text
[măn'-yə-skrĭpt']

mar   sea
aquamarine: blue-green in color, like
sea water [ăk'-wə-mə-rēn']
marine: of or pertaining to the sea
[mə-rēn']
submarine: being, living, or used
under water [sŭb'-mə-rēn']

memor   remember
commemorate: to honor the memory
of, as by a ceremony [kə-měm'-ə-rāt']
memorable: able to be remembered;
worth remembering [měm'-ə-rə-bəl]
memorial: related to remembering a
person or event [mə-môr'-ē-əl]
memorization: the process of
committing something to memory
[měm'-ə-rə-zā'-shən]
memorize: to learn something so
well that you are able to remember it
perfectly [měm'-ə-rīz']
memory: an ability to retain
knowledge; an individual's stock of
retained knowledge [měm'-ə-rē]

miss   send, let go
admission: entry; entrance fee
[əd-mǐ'-shən]
emissary: a representative of a
country or group sent on a mission
[ěm'-ǐ-sěr'-ē]
intermission: interval of time between
periods of activity; a pause
[ǐn'-tər-mǐ'-shən]

mit   send, let go
admit: let enter, give access to
[əd-mǐt']
remit: discharge; pardon; set free,
release [rə-mǐt']

mitt   send, let go
remittance: the act of sending back
money to pay [rǐ-mǐt'-ns]

mob   move
immobile: motionless; unable to move
[ǐ-mō'-bəl]
immobility: relating to the quality of
not being able to move [ǐm-ō-bǐl'-ə-tē]
mobile: relating to being able to move;
movable [mō'-bəl]
mobility: relating to the quality of
being able to move [mō-bǐl'-ə-tē]

mot   move
commotion: the scene of noisy
confusion or activity [kə-mō'-shən]
promotion: an advancement in rank
or position [prə-mō'-shən]

mote   move
promote: to move forward or raise to
a higher rank, class, status, etc.
[prə-mōt]

mov   move
immovable: unable to move or be
moved; fixed; immobile [ǐ-mōō'-və-bəl]
movable: able to be moved from one
place to another [mōō'-və-bəl]
removable: able to be taken or carried
away [rǐ-mōō'-və-bəl]

nom   name, law, custom, order
misnomer: an error in naming a
person or thing [mǐs-nō'-mər]

nomin   name, law, custom, order
nominal: being something in name
only but not in reality [nŏm'-ə-nəl]
nominally: in name only; in a very
small amount [nŏm'-ə-nə-lē]
nomination: action of choosing
someone for a position, office, etc.
[nŏm'-ə-nā'-shən]

nov   new
innovate: to introduce new methods,
devices, etc. [ǐn'-ə-vāt']
innovation: a new idea, method, or
device [ǐn'-ə-vā'-shən]
novelist: one who writes novels
[nŏv'-ə-lǐst]
novelty: newness, originality
[nŏv'-əl-tē]
novice: a person who is new to an
activity; a beginner [nŏv'-ǐs]
renovate: to make something like new
again [rěn'-ə-vāt']
renovation: the action or process of
making something like new again
[rěn'-ə-vā'-shən]

pose place, put
compose: to put together or arrange in proper order [kəm-pōz']
expose: to place something where it can be seen; to put in an unprotected situation [ĭk-spōz']
impose: to put an excessive or unjust burden on someone [ĭm-pōz']
oppose: to act in opposition to; to put against [ə-pōz']

posit place, put
composition: an arrangement or putting together of parts [kŏm'-pə-zĭsh'-ən]
deposit: to put down or in a safe place [dĭ-pŏz'-ĭt]
deposition: the act of putting down or depositing; the removing from power [dĕ-pə-zi'-shən]
exposition: a writing or speaking that puts forth or explains [ĕk'-spə-zish'-ən]
imposition: an excessive or unjust burden placed on someone [ĭm'-pə-zĭsh'-ən]
opposition: the act of resistance or action against [ŏp'-ə-zĭsh'-ən]

pug fight
pugilism: the act of boxing [pyoo'-jə-lĭz-əm]
pugilist: one who fights as a profession; boxer [pyoo'-jə-lĭst]

pugn fight
pugnacious: having a quarrelsome or aggressive nature [pŭg-nā'-shəs]
repugnant: distasteful; offensive or revolting [rĭ-pŭg'-nənt]

rupt to break, burst
corrupt: to cause to break with what is legally or morally right [kə-rupt']
corruption: a break with what is legally or morally right [kə-rup'-shən]
interrupt: to stop or hinder by breaking in on [ĭn'-tə-rŭpt']
interruption: action of stopping or hindering by breaking in on [ĭn'-tə-rŭp'-shən]
rupture: a breaking apart or the state of being broken apart [rŭp'-chər]

scrib write, written
indescribable: not able to be described [ĭn-də-skrī'-bə-bəl]

scribe write, written
circumscribe: to draw around; to encircle [sur'-kəm-skrīb']
describe: to represent with words or pictures [dĭ-skrīb']
inscribe: to write or engrave on some surface [ĭn-skrīb']
prescribe: to write or set down as a rule, order, or direction; to order or advise as a medicine [prĭ-skrīb']

script write, written
circumscriptive: tending to limit or enclose; restrictive [sûr'-kəm-skrĭp'-tĭv]
description: action or process of picturing in words [də-skrĭp'-shən]
descriptive: tending to put forth in words [də-skrĭp'-tĭv]
inscription: an engraving on a coin or other object [ĭn-skrĭp'-shən]
manuscript: a handwritten document or author's original text [măn'-yə-skrĭpt']
postscript: an addition to an already completed letter, article, or book [pōst'-skrĭpt']
prescription: a written order for medicine [prĭ-skrĭp'-shən]

sect cut
dissect: to cut apart piece by piece [dī-sĕkt']
dissection: an analysis part by part, a detailed examination [dī-sĕk'-shən]
intersect: to cut across, traverse [ĭn'-tər-sĕkt']
intersection: the place or point where two things cross each other [ĭn'-tər-sĕk'-shən]

son sound
dissonance: lack of harmony; discord [dĭs'-ə-nəns]
dissonant: charcterized by a lack of harmony; discordant [dĭs'-ə-nənt]
ultrasonic: related to a frequency of sound vibrations beyond the normal hearing range; high frequency [ŭl'-trə-sŏn'-ĭk]
unison: as one voice [yoo'-nĭ-sən]

spec look, examine
specification: the process of stating in detail; requirement; stipulation [spĕs'-ə-fĭ-kā'-shən]
specify: to describe in detail [spĕs'-ə-fī']

spect look, examine

inspect: to examine, to look over carefully [ĭn-spĕkt']

inspection: the act of examining or reviewing [ĭn-spĕk'-shən]

retrospect: the remembering of past events [rĕt'-rə-spĕkt']

retrospection: the act of looking back on past events, experiences, etc. [rĕ'-trə-spĕk'-shən]

retrospective: looking back on the past or past events [rĕ'-trə-spĕk'-tĭv]

struct build

construct: to form by putting together parts [kən-strŭkt']

construction: the action or process of building [kən-strŭkt'-shən]

destruct: to deliberately destroy an object [dĭ-strŭkt']

destruction: the act of destroying; a state of damage [dĭ-strŭk'-shən]

infrastructure: underlying framework of a system [ĭn'-frə-strŭk'-chər]

obstruct: to block or fill with obstacles [əb-strŭkt']

obstruction: an obstacle or something put up against something else [əb-strŭk'-shən]

reconstruct: to put back together again [rē'-kən-strŭkt']

reconstruction: the act of putting back together [rē'-kən-strŭk'-shən]

structure: that which is built in a particular way [strŭk'-chər]

tact touch

contact: the state of touching or meeting [kŏn'-tăkt']

intact: with nothing missing; left whole [ĭn-tăkt']

tactile: of or relating to the sense of touch [tăk'-təl]

tempor time

contemporaneously: having the quality of existing, occurring, or originating at the same time [kən-tĕm'-pə-rā'-nē-əs-lē]

contemporary: of the same time; modern time [kən-tĕm'-pə-rĕr'-ē]

extemporaneous: done without preparation; impromptu [ĭk-stĕm'-pə-rā'-nē-əs]

extemporaneously: in a spur of the moment manner [ĭk-stĕm'-pə-rā'-nē-əs-lē]

temporal: of, or related to a limited time as opposed to eternity; temporary [tĕm'-pə-rəl]

temporary: lasting for a limited time [tĕm'-pə-rĕr'-ē]

termin end, limit

determination: an intent to reach a goal [dĭ-tûr'-mə-nā'-shən]

exterminate: to destroy or get rid of completely [ĭk-stûr'-mə-nāt']

extermination: process of destroying or getting rid of completely [ĭk-stûr'-mə-nā'-shən]

terminal: related to something leading to the end or to death [tûr'-mə-nəl]

terminate: to bring to an end [tûr'-mə-nāt']

tort twist

contort: to twist from its usual shape or position [kən-tôrt']

contortion: a twisted shape or position [kən-tôr'-shən]

distort: to alter the shape or condition of [dĭ-stôrt']

distortion: the process of altering the shape or condition of [dĭ-stôr'-shən]

tract to draw or pull, drag, draw out

contract: to draw together [kən-trăkt]

contraction: act of drawing together or shrinking [kən-trăk'-shən]

extract: to pull or draw out from [ĭk-străkt']

extractible: able to be pulled or drawn out from [ĭk-străk'-tə-bəl]

extraction: process of withdrawing, pulling out [ĭk-străk'-shən]

retract: to draw or pull back [rĭ-trăkt']

retraction: process of pulling back [rək-trăk'-shən]

vene come

convene: to meet together; assemble [kən-vēn]

intervene: to come between; to intercede [ĭn'-tər-vēn']

vent come

circumvent: to go around; to bypass restrictions [sûr'-kəm-vĕnt']

circumvention: process of going around; the act of bypassing restrictions [sûr'-kəm-vĕn'-chən]

circumventive: tending to go around; tending to bypass restrictions [sûr'-kəm-vĕn'tiv]

convent: religious house where a community of nuns reside [kŏn'-vənt]

convention: a gathering or assembly of people with a common interest [kən-věn'-chən]

intervention: the action of coming between; act of interceding [ĭn'-tər-věn'-chən]

ver   truth

veracious: having the quality of being honest; truthful [və-rā'-shəs]

veracity: truth, honesty [və-răs'-ĭ-tē]

verification: the process of confirming the truth [věr'-ə-fĭ-kā'-shən]

veritable: being in fact the true or real thing; actual [věr'-ə-tə-bəl]

vers   turn

aversion: the act of turning away from; a dislike of something [ə-vûr'-zhən]

conversion: a change from one thing, state, or religion to another [kən-vûr'-zhən]

extroversion: turning outward; focusing on others [ěk'-strə-vûr'-zhən]

introversion: turning inward; focusing on oneself [ĭn'-trə-vûr'-zhən]

verse   turn

traverse: to move across or turn back and forth across [trə-vûrs']

vert   turn

avert: to turn away; to keep from happening [ə-vûrt']

convert: to turn into or transform [kən-vûrt']

extrovert: an outgoing person [ěk'-strə-vûrt']

introvert: a person whose interest is more in himself than in others [ĭn'-trə-vûrt']

invert: to turn inside out or upside down [ĭn-vûrt']

vinc   conquer

convincible: able to be conquered; able to be made to agree with [kən-vĭn'-sə-bəl]

invincible: unbeatable; impossible to overcome [ĭn-vĭn'-sə-bəl]

vince   conquer

convince: to persuade by argument or evidence [kən-vĭns']

vis   see

envision: to picture in the mind [ěn-vĭzh'-ən]

visible: able to be seen [vĭz'-ə-bəl]

invisible: impossible to see [ĭn-vĭz'-ə-bəl]

viv   live, life

convivial: lively, jovial, friendly [kən-vĭv'-ē-əl]

revival: the act of bringing back to life; renewed interest in [rĭ-vī'-vəl]

vivacious: high-spirited and full of life [vĭ-vā'-shəs]

vivaciously: done in a high-spirited manner [vĭ-vā'-shəs-lē]

vivid: in a bright or intense manner [vĭv'-ĭd]

vividly: lively in appearance; vigorous [vĭv'-ĭd-lē]

vive   live, life

revive: to bring back to life or consciousness [rə-vīv']

voc   voice, call

equivocate: to use misleading language that could be interpreted two different ways [ĭ-kwĭv'-ə-kāt']

irrevocable: not subject to reversal [ĭ-rě'-və-kə-bəl]

revocable: able to be repealed or withdrawn [rěv'-ə-kə-bəl]

vocalize: to put into words, to utter, to speak [vō'-kə-līz]

vocation: calling, profession, career [vō-kā'-shən]

voci   voice, call

vociferous: loud, noisy [vō-sĭf'-ər-əs]

vol   will, wish

benevolence: the act of doing good; kindliness [bə-něv'-ə-lənts]

benevolent: showing kindness or goodwill [bə-něv'-ə-lənt]

volition: the act of making a choice or decision [və-lĭsh'-ən]

vor   eat

carnivorous: flesh-eating [kŏr-nĭv'-ər-əs]

herbivorous: plant-eating [hûr-bĭv'-ər-əs]

voracious: desiring or eating food in great quantities [vô-rā'-shəs]

vour   eat

devour: to eat quickly [dĭ-vour']

Latin Suffixes

-able able to be
durable: having the quality of lasting [door'-ə-bəl]
immovable: unable to move or be moved; fixed; immobile [ĭ-mōō'-və-bəl]
indescribable: not able to be described [ĭn-də-skrī'-bə-bəl]
irrevocable: not subject to reversal [ĭ-rĕ'-və-kə-bəl]
memorable: able to be remembered; worth remembering [mĕm'-ə-rə-bəl]
movable: able to be moved from one place to another [mōō'-və-bəl]
processable: able to be subjected to a series of actions that yield a change [prŏ'-sĕ-sə-bəl]
removable: able to be taken or carried away [rĭ-mōō'-və-bəl]
revocable: able to be repealed or withdrawn [rĕv'-ə-kə-bəl]

it-able able to be
equitable: fair; just [ĕk'-wĭ-tə-bəl]
veritable: being in fact the true or real thing; actual [vĕr'-ə-tə-bəl]

-acious having the quality of
loquacious: very talkative [lō-kwā'-shəs]
loquaciously: in a very talkative or wordy manner [lō-kwā'-shəs-lē]
loquaciousness: the quality of being very talkative [lō-kwā'-shəs-nəs]
pugnacious: having a quarrelsome or aggressive nature [pŭg-nā'-shəs]
veracious: having the quality of being honest; truthful [və-rā'-shəs]
vivacious: high-spirited and full of life [vĭ-vā'-shəs]
vivaciously: done in a high-spirited manner [vĭ-vā'-shəs-lē]
voracious: desiring or eating food in great quantities [vô-ră'-shəs]

-acity the quality of
veracity: truth, honesty [və-răs'-ĭ-tē]

-al like, related to; an action or process
annual: related to a period of one year [ăn'-yoo-əl]
annually: in the manner of occurring once a year [ăn'-yoo-ə-lē]

biannual: happening twice a year [bī-ăn'-yoo-əl]
bilateral: of or involving two sides; reciprocal [bī-lăt'-ər-əl]
fractional: related to being very small; insignificant [frăk'-shən-əl]
fragmental: related to being incomplete or broken [frăg-mĕnt'-əl]
lateral: of or relating to the side [lăt'-ər-əl]
laterally: by, to, or from the side; sideways [lăt'-ər-ə-lē]
manual: having to do with the hands [măn'-yōō-əl]
nominal: being something in name only but not in reality [nŏm'-ə-nəl]
nominally: in name only; in a very small amount [nŏm'-ə-nə-lē]
revival: the act of bringing back to life; renewed interest in [rĭ-vī'-vəl]
terminal: related to something leading to the end or to death [tur'-mə-nəl]
temporal: of, or related to a limited time as opposed to eternity; temporary [tĕm'-pə-rəl]
unilateral: affecting one side of something [yōō'-nə-lăt'-ər-əl]
vocalize: to put into words, to utter, to speak [vō'-kə-līz]

i-al like, related to; an action or process
bicentennial: of or relating to an age or period of 200 years [bī'-sĕn-tĕn'-ē-əl]
centennial: of or relating to an age or period of 100 years [sĕn-tĕn'-ē-əl]
convivial: lively, jovial, friendly [kən-vĭv'-ē-əl]
memorial: related to remembering a person or event [mə-môr'-ē-əl]
perennial: lasting through many years [pə-rĕn'-ē-əl]

-ance state, quality, act
dissonance: lack of harmony; discord [dĭs'-ə-nəns]
remittance: the act of sending money back to pay [rĭ-mĭt'-ns]

-aneous having the quality of

contemporaneously: having the quality of existing, occurring, or originating at the same time [kən-tĕm'-pə-rā'-nē-əs-lē]

extemporaneous: done without preparation; impromptu [ĭk-stĕm'-pə-rā'-nē-əs]

extemporaneously: in a spur of the moment manner [ĭk-stĕm'-pə-rā'-nē-əs-lē]

-ant one who, that which ; state, quality

dissonant: charcterized by a lack of harmony; discordant [dĭs'-ə-nənt]

repugnant: distasteful; offensive or revolting [rĭ-pŭg'-nənt]

iz-ant one who, that which ; state, quality

cognizant: the state of being aware or informed of something [kŏg'-nə-zənt]

-arium place where

aquarium: a place where aquatic organisms are kept and exhibited [ə-kwĕr'-ē-əm]

-ary that which; of, related to ; one who; someone or something that belongs to

aviary: a large enclosure in which birds are kept [ā'-vē-ĕr'-ē]

contemporary: of the same time; modern time [kən-tĕm'-pə-rĕr'-ē]

emissary: a representative of a country or group sent on a mission [ĕm'-ĭ-sĕr'-ē]

fragmentary: not complete; disconnected [frăg'-mən-tĕr'-ē]

luminary: an object, like a star, that gives off light; a famous person (a "star") [lōō'-mə-nĕr-'ē]

temporary: lasting for a limited time [tĕm'-pə-rĕr'-ē]

-ate to make, to act; one who, that which

accelerate: to increase the speed of [ăk-sĕl'-ə-rāt']

accumulate: to gather or pile up little by little [ə-kyōōm'-yə-lāt']

animate: to give spirit, life, motion, or activity to [ăn'-ə-māt']

commemorate: to honor the memory of, as by a ceremony [kə-mĕm'-ə-rāt']

decelerate: to reduce the speed of [dē-sĕl'-ə-rāt']

equate: to make, treat, or regard as equal or equivalent [ē-kwāt']

equivocate: to use misleading language that could be interpreted two different ways [ĭ-kwĭv'-ə-kāt']

exterminate: to destroy or get rid of completely [ĭk-stûr'-mə-nāt']

illuminate: to give light to [ĭ-lōō'-mə-nāt']

inanimate: not filled with life or spirit; motionless [ĭ-nă'-nə-mət]

innovate: to introduce new methods, devices, etc. [ĭn'-ə-vāt']

rejuvenate: to bring back to youthful strength or appearance [rĭ-jōō'-və-nāt']

renovate: to make something like new again [rĕn'-ə-vāt']

terminate: to bring to an end [tûr'-mə-nāt']

i-ate to make, to act; one who, that which

abbreviate: to shorten [ə-brē'-vē-āt']

-ation an action or process

acceleration: the action or process of increasing the speed of [ək-sĕl'-ə-rā'-shən]

deceleration: the action or process of reducing the speed of [dē-sĕl'-ə-rā'-shən]

determination: an intention to reach a goal [dĭ-tûr'-mə-nā'-shən]

duration: the length of time something lasts [dōō-rā'-shən]

equation: a statement of equality [ĭ-kwā'-zhən]

exclamation: an outcry, a shout [ĕk'-sklə-mā'-shən]

extermination: process of destroying or getting rid of completely [ĭk-stûr'-mə-nā'-shən]

formation: process of shaping, forming, or establishing [fôr-mā'-shən]

fragmentation: process of breaking, cracking, or splitting; that which is broken or divided [frăg'-mən-tā'-shən]

illumination: the process of lighting up [ĭ-lōō'-mə-nā'-shən]

innovation: a new idea, method, or device [ĭn'-ə-vā'-shən]

nomination: action of choosing someone for a position, office, etc. [nŏm'-ə-nā'-shən]

proclamation: something announced officially in public [prŏk'-lə-mā'-shən]

renovation: the action or process of making something like new again [rĕn'-ə-vā'-shən]

vocation: calling, profession, career [vō-kā'-shən]

ific-ation　an action or process

specification: the process of stating in detail; requirement; stipulation [spĕs-ə-fĭ-kā'-shən]

verification: the process of confirming the truth [vĕr'-ə-fĭ-kā'-shən]

iz-ation　an action or process

memorization: the process of committing something to memory [mĕm'-ə-rə-zā'-shən]

-cide　kill

herbicide: any chemical used to kill unwanted plants, etc. [hûr'-bə-sīd']

-ence　state, quality, act

benevolence: the act of doing good; kindliness [bə-nĕv'-ə-lənts]

credence: belief; acceptance as true or valid [krēd'-ns]

eloquence: speech that is vivid, fluent, forceful, and graceful [ĕl'-ə-kwənts]

i-ence　state, quality, act

audience: a group of listeners or spectators [ô'-dē-əns]

-ent　one who, that which, like, related to

benevolent: showing kindness or goodwill [bə-nĕv'-ə-lənt]

eloquent: speaking beautifully and forcefully [ĕl'-ə-kwənt]

eloquently: speaking in a vivid, fluent, forceful, and graceful manner [ĕl'-ə-kwənt-lē]

-er　one who, that which

misnomer: an error in naming a person or thing [mĭs-nō'-mər]

-eous　like, having the quality of

aqueous: like, or having the quality of water; water [ā'-kwē-əs]

-escent　becoming, having

luminescent: glowing, luminous [loo'-mə-nĕs'-ənt]

-ferous　producing

vociferous: loud, noisy [vō-sĭf'-ər-əs]

i-fy　to make, to act, to do

specify: describe in detail [spĕs'-ə-fī']

-ible　able to be

accessible: easily entered, approached, or obtained [ək-sĕs'-ə-bəl]

audible: able to be heard [ô'-də-bəl]

convincible: able to be conquered; able to be made to agree with [kən-vĭn'-sə-bəl]

credible: able to be believed; believable; reliable [krĕd'-ə-bəl]

extractible: able to be pulled or drawn out from [ĭk-străk'-tə-bəl]

inaudible: unable to be heard [ĭn-ô'-də-bəl]

incredible: too extraordinary and impossible to believe [ĭn-krĕd'-ə-bəl]

invincible: unbeatable; impossible to overcome [ĭn-vĭn'-sə-bəl]

invisible: impossible to see [ĭn-vĭz'-ə-bəl]

visible: able to be seen [vĭz'-ə-bəl]

-ic　like, related to

ultrasonic: related to a frequency of sound vibrations beyond the normal hearing range; high frequency [ŭl'-trə-sŏn'ĭk]

t-ic　like, related to

aquatic: related to the animals and plants that live in or near water [ə-kwŏt'-ĭk]

-ice　one who, that which

novice: a person who is new to an activity; a beginner [nŏv'-ĭs]

-id　like, related to

vivid: lively in appearance; vigorous [vĭv'-ĭd]

vividly: lively in appearance; vigorous [vĭv'-ĭd-lē]

-ile　like, of, relating to

fragile: easily broken; delicate [frăj'-əl]

immobile: motionless; unable to move [ĭ-mō'-bəl]

juvenile: youthful or childish; immature [joo'-və-nīl']

mobile: relating to being able to move; movable [mō'-bəl]

tactile: of or relating to the sense of touch [tăk'-təl]

-ine   like, related to

aquamarine: blue-green in color, like sea water [ăk'-wə-mə-rēn']

marine: of or pertaining to the sea [mə-rēn']

submarine: being, living, or used under water [sŭb'-mə-rēn']

-ion   an action or process; state, quality, act

abduction: a taking away by force [əb-dŭk'-tion]

admission: entry; entrance fee [əd-mĭ'-shən]

aversion: the act of turning away from; a dislike of something [ə-vûr'-zhən]

circumvention: process of going around; the act of bypassing restrictions [sûr'-kəm-věn'-chən]

commotion: the scene of noisy confusion or activity [kə-mō'-shən]

composition: an arrangement or putting together of parts [kŏm'-pə-zĭsh'-ən]

conclusion: the end or last part [kən-klōō'-zhən]

construction: the action or process of building [kən-strŭkt'-shən]

contortion: a twisted shape or position [kən-tôr'-shən]

contraction: act of drawing together or shrinking [kən-trăk'-shən]

contradiction: an action in opposition to another [kŏn'-trə-dĭk'-shən]

convention: a gathering or assembly of people with a common interest [kən-věn'-shən]

conversion: a change from one thing, state, or religion to another [kən-vûr'-zhən]

corruption: a break with what is legally or morally right [kə-rup'-shun]

deduction: a subtraction of an amount [dĭ-dŭk'-shən]

deposition: the act of putting down or depositing; the removing from power [dě-pə-zi'-shən]

description: action or process of picturing in words [də-skrĭp'-shən]

destruction: the act of destroying; a state of damage [dĭ-strŭk'-shən]

diction: the act or manner of expression in words [dĭk'-shən]

digression: a departure from the main issue, subject, etc. [dī-grěsh'-ən]

dissection: an analysis part by part, a detailed examination [dī-sěk'-shən]

distortion: the process of altering the shape or condition of [dĭ-stôr'-shən]

envision: to picture in the mind [ěn-vĭzh'-ən]

exclusion: a shutting out; rejection [ĭk-sklōō'-zhən]

exposition: a writing or speaking that puts forth or explains [ěk'-spə-zish'-ən]

extraction: process of withdrawing, pulling out [ĭk-străk'-shən]

extroversion: turning outward; focusing on others [ěk'-strə-vûr'-zhən]

fraction: a part or element of a larger whole [frăk'-shən]

fractional: related to being very small; insignificant [frăk'-shən-əl]

imposition: an excessive or unjust burden placed on someone [ĭm'-pə-zĭsh'-ən]

inaction: the state of not doing something that should be done; idleness [ĭ-năk'-shən]

induction: the process of formally installing someone to an office or position [ĭn-dŭk'-shən]

infraction: the act of breaking the limits or rules [ĭn-frăk'-shən]

inscription: an engraving on a coin or other object [ĭn-skrĭp'-shən]

inspection: the act of examining or reviewing [ĭn-spěk'-shən]

interaction: communication between two or more people or things [ĭn'-tər-ăk'-shən]

intermission: interval of time between periods of activity; a pause [ĭn'-tər-mĭ'-shən]

interruption: action of stopping or hindering by breaking in on [ĭn'-tə-rŭp'-shən]

intersection: the place or point where two things cross each other [ĭn'-tər-sěk'-shən]

intervention: the action of coming between; act of interceding [ĭn'-tər-věn'-chən]

introversion: turning inward; focusing on oneself [ĭn'-trə-vûr'-zhən]

obstruction: an obstacle or something put up against something else [əb-strŭk'-shən]

opposition: the act of resistance or action against [ŏp'-ə-zĭsh'-ən]

prediction: a statement foretelling the future [prĭ-dĭk'-shən]

prescription: a written order for medicine [prĭ-skrĭp'-shən]

procession: the act of going forward in an orderly manner [prə-sĕ'-shən]

progression: the process or action of moving forward [prə-grĕ'-shən]

promotion: an advancement in rank or position [prə-mō'-shən]

reaction: a response [rē-ăk'-shən]

reconstruction: the act of putting back together [rē'-kən-strŭk'-shən]

regression: a movement backward to an earlier state [rĭ-grĕsh'-ən]

retraction: process of pulling back [rək-trăk'-shən]

retrospection: the act of looking back on past events, experiences, etc. [rĕ'-trə-spĕk'-shən]

secession: the act of formally withdrawing from a group [sĭ-sĕ'-shən]

seclusion: isolation; a shutting off or keeping away from others [sĭ-klōō'-zhən]

il-ism   a state of being, a quality or act
pugilism: the act of boxing [pyōō'-jə-lĭz-əm]

el-ist   one who
novelist: one who writes novels [nŏv'-ə-lĭst]

il-ist   one who
pugilist: one who fights as a profession; boxer [pyōō'-jə-lĭst]

-ity   state, quality, act
brevity: quality of being brief; shortness in time [brĕv-ĭ-tē]

equanimity: calm temperament, evenness of temper [ē'-kwə-nĭm'-ĭ-tē]

equity: fairness; the state of being just or fair [ĕk'-wĭ-tē]

il-ity   state, quality, act
fragility: state of delicateness [frə-jĭl'-ə-tē]

immobility: relating to the quality of not being able to move [ĭm-ō-bĭl'-ə-tē]

mobility: relating to the quality of being able to move [mō-bĭl'-i-tē]

os-ity   state, quality, act
luminosity: the relative quantity of light; a state of being luminous [lōō'-mə-nŏs'-ə-tē]

-ive   tending to or performing
circumscriptive: tending to limit or enclose; restrictive [sûr'-kəm-skrĭp'-tĭv]

circumventive: tending to go around; tending to bypass restrictions [sûr'-kəm-vĕn'tiv]

conclusive: that which settles a question; decisive; final [kən-klōō'-siv]

deductive: tending to use logic or reason to form a conclusion [dĭ-dŭk'-tĭv]

descriptive: tending to put forth in words [də-skrĭp'-tĭv]

exclusive: shutting or ruling out other options, tending to shut out others [ĭk-sklōō'-siv]

interceptive: tending to stop or interrupt the course of [ĭn'-tər-sĕp'-tĭv]

receptive: tending to receive; take in, admit, contain [rə-sĕp'-tĭv]

retrospective: looking back on the past or past events [rĕ'-trə-spĕk'-tĭv]

at-ive   tending to or performing
cumulative: gradually building up [kyōōm'-yə-lə'-tĭv]

illuminative: tending to produce light [ĭ-lōō'-mə-nə-tĭv]

it-ive   tending to or performing
cognitive: having intellectual activity, as in thinking and reasoning [kŏg'-nə-tĭv]

-ize   to make, to act
memorize: to learn something so well that you are able to remember it perfectly [mĕm'-ə-rīz']

recognize: to identify someone or something seen before [rĕk'-əg-nīz']

vocalize: to put into words, to utter, to speak [vō'-kə-līz]

-ly   in the manner of; having the quality of
annually: in the manner of occurring once a year [ăn'-yoo-ə-lē]

contemporaneously: having the quality of existing, occurring, or originating at the same time [kən-tĕm'-pə-rā'-nē-əs-lē]

eloquently: speaking in a vivid, fluent, forceful, and graceful manner [ĕl'-ə-kwənt-lē]

extemporaneously: in a spur of the moment manner [ĭk-stĕm'-pə-rā'-nē-əs-lē]

laterally: by, to, or from the side; sideways [lăt'-ər-ə-lē]

loquaciously: in a very talkative or wordy manner [lō-kwā'-shəs-lē]

nominally: in name only; in a very small amount [nŏm'-ə-nə-lē]

vivaciously: done in a high-spirited manner [vĭ-vā'-shəs-lē]

vividly: lively in appearance; vigorous [vĭv'-ĭd-lē]

-ment   that which; state, quality, act

fragment: a broken piece [frăg'-mənt]

fragmental: related to being incomplete or broken [frăg-mĕnt'-əl]

fragmentary: not complete; disconnected [frăg'-mən-tĕr'-ē]

fragmentation: process of breaking, cracking, or splitting; that which is broken or divided [frăg'-mən-tā'-shən]

-ness   state of being

loquaciousness: the quality of being very talkative [lō-kwā'-shəs-nəs]

-or   one who, that which; condition, state, activity

interceptor: a person or thing that stops or interrupts the course of [ĭn'-tər-sĕp'-tər]

receptor: that which holds or receives (in various senses) [rə-sĕp'-tər]

at-or   one who, that which; condition, state, activity

aviator: one who flies an airplane; pilot [ā'-vē-ā'-tər]

-ous   having the quality of

carnivorous: flesh-eating [kŏr-nĭv'-ər-əs]

herbivorous: plant-eating [hûr-bĭv'-ər-əs]

luminous: giving off or reflecting light [loo'-mə-nəs]

-tion   state, quality, act

aviation: the act or practice of flying airplanes, helicopters, etc. [ā'-vē-ā'-shən]

extraction: process of withdrawing, pulling out [ĭk-străk'-shən]

retraction: process of pulling back [rək-trăk'-shən]

i-tion   state, quality, act

cognition: process of acquiring knowledge [kŏg-nĭsh'-ən]

recognition: act of acknowledging or noticing [rĕ'-kĭg-nĭsh'-ən]

volition: the act of making a choice or decision [və-lĭsh'-ən]

-trix   feminine

aviatrix: a female airplane pilot [ā'-vē-ā'-trĭks]

el-ty   state, quality; that which

novelty: newness, originality [nŏv'-əl-tē]

-ulous   having the quality of

credulous: believing too readily; gullible [krĕj'-ə-ləs]

incredulous: disbelieving; not believing [ĭn-krĕj'-ə-ləs]

-ure   state, quality, act; that which; process, condition

capture: the act of taking or being taken by force [kăp'-chər]

fracture: a break, crack, or split [frăk'-chər]

infrastructure: underlying framework of a system [ĭn'-frə-strŭk'-chər]

recapture: the taking back of something [rē-kăp'-chər]

rupture: a breaking apart or the state of being broken apart [rŭp'-chər]

structure: that which is built in a particular way [strŭk'-chər]

-us   thing which

cumulus: a heap, a pile, a mass; a thick, puffy type of cloud [kyoom'-yə-ləs]

-y   state, quality, act; body, group

memory: an ability to retain knowledge; an individual's stock of retained knowledge [mĕm'-ə-rē]